COPYRIGHT © 2022
Gwen Collins Womack

ALL RIGHTS RESERVED. NO PART OF THIS BOOK MAY BE REPRODUCED, SCANNED, OR DISTRIBUTED IN ANY PRINTED OR ELECTRONIC FORM WITHOUT PERMISSION OF THE PUBLISHER.

PLEASE DO NOT PARTICIPATE, ENCOURAGE PIRACY OF COPYRIGHTED MATERIALS IN VIOLATION OF THE AUTHOR'S AND PUBLISHER'S RIGHTS.

PURCHASE ONLY AUTHORIZED EDITIONS.

ISBN: 978-0-578-38607-2
EISBN: 978-0-578-38608-9

EDITED BY:
LYNDA RAHEEM
SONYA RAHEEM-DAVIS

Publisher:
BAGAWAI STUDIO PRESS, Inc. for
Andre Ricardo, Inc.

WWW.ANDRERICARDO.COM

EDITOR'S NOTE

FOUR is the fourth installment in Gwen Womack's incredibly fascinating life from the small-town setting of Madisonville, Kentucky to the relatively larger city of Charleston, West Virginia. The journey took her from the safety of her grandmother's home to the bordello's of Charleston's seedy side streets to a prison revolt, where a lacerated Gwen is swinging a fireplace poker at five armed and locked state troopers. As with the other volumes in this series, you're in for a wild ride. Grab some popcorn, a warm blanket and a comfy chair because Gwen Womack is back!

*** . *** . ***

There are a couple of clarifications I need to offer, in terms of the formatting of her story. "Chapter 1" of each book is our TEASER chapter. In other words, it's just a glimpse of a moment that you'll find in the book. Chronologically, Gwen's story picks up from the previous book in Chapter Two.

Additionally, we originally planned to have Gwen's daring and inexplicably exciting memoir to be spread over the course of six books. We've decided to combine the planned books for FIVE and SIX into just one final book, which will be called, FIVE. (Subtitled: In The Free World Doing Time)

For your convenience, every book in the series will now have an accompanying ebook.

Lastly, books ONE, TWO, and THREE will undergo a minor transformation and be re-released as a "Revised Edition."

*** *** ***

There are many, many people I would love to thank in the production of this edition, but I am profoundly happy to thank our former county commissioner for District 8, and Mrs. Steff Solovei and the Neighbors And Neighbors Association, Inc. for their generous support to our publishing company. Thank you, so very, very much.

I would be at a loss without thanking Mrs. Juliette Ross and M Publications for giving us the opportunity to represent Gwen's story.

BOOK FIVE will be published in July, 2022.

Be safe, keep reading and God bless!

Andre

DEDICATION

I dedicate this work to myself for enduring when I wanted to quit so many times. I am thankful for my daddy's DNA that would not let me quit.

I dedicate this work to my husband, WEST WOMACK, for loving me for 35 years through it all.

I dedicate this work to Mr. Andre Lawrence, my publisher, who didn't question who, what, when, where or how but worked with me tirelessly until the work was done.

Finally, I dedicated BOOK #4 to all who will read and recognize it isn't over until God says it is over.

Gwen
December 25, 2021

1
THE TEASER

A few minutes passed and Gwen heard the expected grumblings inside the bedroom. She slowly got up and went through the secret door to the basement.

As far as the eye could see, the darkly lit room was cluttered with books, papers and boxes. Old paintings with inch-high dust adorned all four walls. The images, mostly faded with time, seemed to be direct relations with Mister Jim. She looked around frantically for the big box and the bag underneath but the jitters had her second-guessing her purpose. She took a deep breath and closed her eyes. She slowly opened them and saw the box and the bag.

She was tempted to look inside first, but wondered if she were caught with the opened box, could it spell time in Pence again.

She carefully crept up the stairs and as she was about to reach the top step, she noticed another bag, off in the corner. She felt the pull to see what was in that bag.

She got to the car and threw the bag in the backseat. When she got back in the foyer, she leaned into the bedroom door and it sounded like Vicky was finishing up. She knew it was now or never. She threw caution to the wind and raced downstairs.

This bag was noticeably heavier and bulkier than she reasoned. She heard the sound of metal rubbing against metal. Whatever was in there, she had to find out. Besides that, as she carefully picked up the bag, she realized that she was never coming back. So in the end, it wouldn't matter.

The women made it back to Gwen's motel and were lucky enough to find a parking space right in front of the door. Gwen carried the lighter bag and Vicky struggled with the last bag.

The squealing sound of a whistle echoed in the empty hallway. Then it happened again.

Gwen had trouble opening her eyes. She didn't know if it was because she was drowsy or the weight of her still-swollen eyes. She moved her head as if it were a nightmare she was trying to elude.

There was silence for a moment, followed by a heavy thud against the door.

"COLLINS!" Three heavy thuds followed in quick succession. "COLLINS… WE'RE COMING IN!"

She wiped her eyes slowly then lifted herself up but was slumped when the door opened.

It was still pitch-black but in the shard of moonlight that came from outside her window, she was able to see one of the nurses remove the key from the lock and placed it back in a pouch on her waist.

"Collins… It's time to go!" There was silence. "I need you to get up… NOW!"

"Wha… why? I didn't do anything," Gwen said as she fought to keep her eyes open.

"Collins, we didn't say you did anything. We need you to get up right now! That's an order. Get up. Wash your face and collect your things," the other nurse interjected. "NOW, COLLINS!"

Gwen was now fully awake, but she still felt a bit disoriented. She looked around the room and it was just as she left it before she went asleep except now there were two nurses standing in front of her bed.

She crept out of bed and attempted to fix the cover when she noticed one of the nurses shaking her head in disapproval.

"Where am I going," she said as she adjusted her feet in her sandals.

"Gather all of your things, Collins. You won't be returning. Wash your face and don't forget to pack all of your things. We have to go right now."

Her heart raced when she saw the stern, blank expression on the faces of the nurses. She wondered what time it was, but judging from her window, it still had to be several hours before daybreak.

A few shorts minutes later, Gwen found herself downstairs watching several nurses talking in a low voice to two Pence guards as Buffy stood nearby shivering and crying.

The Pence guards said nothing to Gwen when they made eye-contact with her but one of the guards took the pad that the receptionist had push through the slat underneath the window and signed it on several different pages.

"Collins," one of the Pence officers said. "Turn around and place your hands behind your back."

Gwen wanted to say something but quickly remembered that this was the behavior that got her and the other inmates in trouble in the first place. The other Pence officer held on to Buffy and when Gwen was secured, the officers gently tugged them to walk out of the front door.

One of the officers unlocked and opened the backseat door, "Remember your rights, inmates. You're still under arrest and any further infractions, verbal or otherwise, can and will result in additional jail time. Do you understand me?"

"Yes, officer," Gwen and Buffy said in unison, in a low voice.

"And, one more thing. You had better be quiet when we get back. It would not be in your best interest to let the Warden find out that you've been talking about matters with the other inmates that don't concern them. Do I make myself abundantly clear, inmates?"

"Yes, ma'am," they both replied.

3

It felt surreal to Gwen. She was both excited and scared at the same time as the car slowed down and turned into the driveway at Pence. She felt the adrenaline and the fatigue of being awake at 4:32 in the morning.

The trip was less than two hours long but somehow she felt as if she were in a time-capsule and that something was awaiting her. The feeling gripped her soul.

Buffy's grip on Gwen's arm tighten as the car slowly came to a stop. Her breath became shorter but faster. She wanted to speak when Gwen turned around to look at her. Gwen nodded to her. She nodded back very slowly.

One of the guards opened the door closest to the entrance doorway and helped them out, while the other guard took their bags from the trunk.

"Okay," One of the guards said, "walk directly to your rooms. Don't look or speak to anyone you see. Do you hear me?" Turning to Gwen, "Collins, that means you!"

Gwen stared at her for a moment, knowing she had to resist the temptation to answer her back but deep inside herself she knew the consequence of back-talking a Pence guard was an additional 6-month setback." "Yes, ma'am."

Gwen came out first and noticed all of the lights on the main floor as well as on the second and third floors. She saw shadows moving around, one tall one looking at them from behind the main door.

The entrance door opened to the main foyer revealing a cue of Pence officers standing in a row against the wall leading up to the staircase. In the middle stood a conspicuously dressed man that Gwen had never seen before. He wore a dark blue suit with a badge clipped to the upper left jacket pocket. He also had a whistle hanging from a small chain around his neck. He didn't smile and only his eyes moved as the women walked past him. Who was this man, Gwen thought. And, where was Warden Blankenship? Gwen tried her best to not make eye-contact but this tall man, with salt and pepper hair stood stoic with his arms crossed just above his midsection. Whatever his purpose for being there, Gwen surmised, she knew he was aware of the situation.

Gwen, with Buffy walking quickly behind her, looked only at the staircase in front of her that led up to their rooms. They could feel the heat from the guards' expressionless stares but nothing as intense as the new guy. As she passed the last of the guards, who stood in cue. She noticed a new guard. In fact, she was the last one. The woman, a black woman was looking at her and smiling.

Gwen hesitated for a second and turned to her. She was happy to see this new guard was an African-American. She smiled back and resumed her stride as she walked up the stairs.

*** *** ***

Gwen opened the door to her room. It was unlocked as the guards said. The room was a disaster: clothes, shoes and papers all over of the place. She looked around and saw the box where she kept all of the letters she received, especially from her mother and great aunt. It took a little while but she slowly remembered what her room used to look like. She thought for a moment but decided that she couldn't go to sleep with the room in that state of chaos.

The room was cold, dark and empty. She heard the door close behind her, the lock engaged. She slowly turned around in a circle. It looked familiar but it wasn't. Even by her standards, the room felt different. It smelled different. In the stillness, she felt the lingering presence of the police.

She stooped down to place her palms on the floor. Gently touching the surface, she felt both the cracks and the grout that sealed the tiles around it. Slowly, she gathered the clothes around her and folded each garment into small piles of like items. The gestures stirred memories of the last moment she had in that very spot. She was in the very spot where the thunder of bangs broke the locks on the door just a few feet away.

She crawled a few feet, staring at the floor hoping to see some reminder of the past. She remembered seeing a flash of blue, then the sound of circle of black patent boots and the screams that came with it.

She stared at the spot, replayed the moment a boot was so near her face that she was able to see the stitching. She ignored the screams and hid her hands underneath her when the officers reached for her hands. She responded to the screams with her own. This happened until the weight of a fist came down on the side of her face.

She touched the right temple and recalled feeling the area where the skin separated. The first blow pushed her head a few inches.

The second followed immediately, then a third. Her vision was blurred by the blood that seeped in from the side. She lost sight of his fist from the glare of the light above him, only seeing it just before impact.

She held her eyes, feeling the bloating extended from one corner of her eye to the other, just above the cheek bone and above the eye-brow. In the midst of the storm, she could hear one of the female guards screaming at her from a distance pleading with her to stay still and not hold on to the trooper's pant leg.

Gwen was in a daze, the memory of that moment revisited her like her worst nightmare was standing before her smiling and waving.

Her mind snapped to the present. Taking a deep breath, she looked at a spot on the ground and realized she was hovering over the place where she recalled, with her good eye, were the dozens of small reflections of her face screaming in terror.

As hard as she stared at the floor, there was no way she could ever forget how close to death she was at that moment. She had escaped death yet again, but the epiphany was bitter sweet because she knew once again she put herself in harm's way and she had no one to blame but herself.

Gwen turned around and laid on the floor. She didn't want to let the memory fade from her imagination by sleeping on her bed. At least for one night.

"Gwen…Gwen…"

The sound of her name slowly brought Gwen to the present. She struggled to fully open her eyes while her vision was still blurry.

"Gwen… Gwen Collins, are you all right? What are you doing on the floor," the voice above her said.

Slowly, the mid-afternoon sunlight welcomed her back to the old life at Pence. She took a deep breath and tried to make out who this beautiful, black woman in a white blouse and Prussian-blue, pleated shirt that dropped just below her knees.

"Miss Collins… are you all right? Would you like to go to the infirmary?" Gwen shook her head slightly. She opened her mouth but the edges felt as if they hadn't been opened in years. She lifted her hands to her face and gently rubbed her eyes. Her mind started churning, *Who is this lady? Where do I know this lady from? Was she one of my teachers from Charleston or a neighbor?*

The woman knelt down and offered her a hand. "Do you want to get up?"

Gwen slowly lifted herself upward and sat straight up.

The guard looked at her, "Hi Gwen, I heard all about you. I'm Officer Huffman. It's nice to finally meet you."

She shook her head, "Hi…uhh… do I know you?"

"No, we're just meeting. I saw you when you came in this morning. Officer Bowling told me all about you. She told me that you're special although your mouth sometimes get you into trouble. And, she told me that I should look after you because you really don't belong here."

Gwen looked at her. "She said that? She really said that!"

"Yes, she did. She also told me that you have a bright future."

"I thought Mrs. Bowling was mad at me... I... I ...I thought she'd never speak to me again."

"Believe me, she cares for you a lot. Here, let me help you up. You shouldn't sleep on the floor. It's not good for your back."

Officer Huffman helped Gwen to the bed. She stood by the foot of the bed looking at Gwen. "She also told me everything that happened that night. She knows that you didn't mean to hit her. She said you were scared when you saw the troopers coming at you."

"I am so...so...sorry. Ms. Bowling is my friend and I would never do anything to hurt her."

"Gwen, we both want to help you but you've got to follow instructions. The rules are there to protect you. We don't want anything else to happen to you but you must follow directions. I was sent to help the new warden understand our... experiences. I've got to tell you, Gwen, after being here a few weeks and seeing some of the other women from Charleston, I think you have the best shot at not returning. But, you've got to work closely with me and Ms. Bowling. That's the only way to stay out of trouble."

"I can't have people talking crazy to me. I just can't."

"Well…you're going to have to make a decision about your future. You can either follow directions and stay out of trouble or you can continue down this path and spend a few more years here. It's up to you." Officer Huffman turned and walked toward the door.

"Officer Huffman, can I ask you one more question?"

"Yes. I'm listening."

"Did they ever find out what happened that night?"

Officer Huffman took a deep breath and turned around, "They found out who took the officer's money… and they dealt with it. They know you had nothing to do with it."

Gwen looked down at her hands. She heard Ms. Huffman walk out and the door close behind her.

One morning, when wiping away the fog from the bathroom mirror, she still saw the tiny imprint of the trooper's fraternal order ring around her eye socket. She thought to herself, This is my scarlet letter.

None of the inmates from Charleston spoke to her at first. Whenever she would see Terri, Terri would return a silent, grim stare to Gwen's hopeful smile. Still, Gwen always walked around her table peering around to the other tables, wishing to make eye-contact with anyone. She thought to herself, if anyone would return the look, then maybe she'd have a chance to reconnect with a group.

She looked at her plate and slowly sliced the piece of custard pie with the side of her fork.

"You know, you should eat your vegetables first or at least have a portion of veggies and meat together then when you're finished, you can have dessert. It'll digest better."

Gwen looked up and saw Mrs. Huffman standing over her smiling. She suddenly found herself smiling back.

"Misses Huffman, sit!"

"No, Gwen, I'm sorry, I can't. I have to make the rounds. I just wanted to come by and check on you."

"I'm doing fine. Thanks for asking!"

"Gwen, I know the woman needed some time to warm up to you but I told them to let bygones be bygones. Terri is leaving soon and will be going back to her life in Charleston. I told her that I was hoping that she talk to you and get out everything that she's keeping in."

"I don't know what she's mad about. I'm the one who got hit and I wasn't even the one who stole that woman's money."

"Gwen, I know that and you know that. But, that's beside the point. I know you and her were really good friends. Just hear me out. Clear the air and when you're done with your time, you may find that the woman who was your friend that rainy night a few years ago is still your friend today."

Gwen rolled her eyes.

"I didn't say it would be easy but it'll be easy but it'll give you the chance to break the ice."

"Okay, I'll hear what she has to say but I still don't believe it was all my fault."

"I understand. So I can count on you not feeling threatened if she approaches you."

"No, Mrs. Huffman. I won't let it aggravate me."

"Okay, then. I have to finish my rounds. I'll be around to check on you later."

Gwen said nothing but slowly ate as she watched Mrs. Huffman walk away in the distance.

All of this talk reminded her of Buffy.

She had only seen Buffy a few times after they returned but not before Buffy was paroled. She hoped Buffy would, at least, write to let her know she was okay and to let her know how things were outside of Pence.

But, no letter ever came. Nothing. It would be last time she ever heard from her. She took this a s a sign that Buffy may have blamed her too for everything that went down.

She finished her meal and dropped off the tray. She walked slowly toward the stairs going up when she remembered the empty room where she used to go to find solace.

To her surprise, the room was open and nothing was missing. *That's strange, she thought. I just knew they wouldn't let me in this place after all the trouble I caused.*

She walked around the room, fascinated that nothing was removed. Something caught her eye in the corner. There it was, she hoped it wasn't gone, but no, there it stood: the small, two-speaker radio. She quickly turned it on, turning the dial until she heard something familiar. Within a moment, she began to sing the female parts. This, she thought, was like old times.

Before she knew it, she had been singing for hours. She looked at the old clock on the wall just above the window. She stared at it for a moment. It seemed as if time had stood still. It had, in fact, the clock wasn't working.

She remembered a conversation she had with her grandmother. She told Gwen, "A broken clock is right twice a day. When you get a second chance, don't let it go. Learn from your mistakes and don't let it happen again!"

"Gwen, when you're finished the dishes, I need you over here to cut these onions. The girl who was supposed to do this in the infirmary."

"Okay, no problem."

"When you're done, I've got a few extra bag of Doritos on the shelf, help yourself… but this is a one-time thing."

"Thank you!"

Gwen finished her duties a short time afterwards. She sat on a chair and slowly put one chip in her mouth at a time. The thoughts of the past couple of days kept revolving in her mind. Had she learned her lessons and would she keep a low profile? Would she stand up for her rights because she was no one's fool? How much time would she have added to her sentence if she were to defend herself in a fight?

"Collins…Collins…wake up, stop daydreaming! This ain't your room." Terri stood in front of her holding a tray with dirty plate with a half-eaten sandwich on it.

Gwen stood up and stared back at Terri without saying a word.

"So what you got to say for yourself? Don't think I forgot about you."

"What you want me to say?"

Terri stared harder into her eyes.

"Okay. I'm sorry."

Terri said nothing but dapped around the area of Gwen's eye with a cold, damp cloth.

A couple of inmates were walking by when then recognized Gwen's voice. Peeking in the doorway, one of them blurted out, "You're sorry! You're sorry! That's all you got to say? I'm sorry. You know what you put us through?"

"How was I supposed to know Crawford was going to call the fuzz," Gwen answered back.

"Why couldn't you just keep your big mouth shut?"

Gwen was about to walk away when she stopped and turned back around, "What have I ever done to you except been good to you? You seem to have forgotten that I brought you home when you were sitting on the steps in the rain. I let you stay with me when you had nobody else."

"If it hadn't been for you running your mouth," the second woman said as she pointed her finger in Gwen's face, "none of this would've happen. If you would've just shut the hell up, none of us would have gotten extra time."

"I'm sorry. I'm really, really sorry. I was just doing what I thought was right. I thought I was fighting for our rights. I didn't know this would happen."

"That's just like you, Collins, only thinking about yourself. You could've gotten us killed. Those crackers don't give a F about us."

"I don't know what else to tell you. I'm sorry and I just want us to be cool, even if you don't want to be friends."

Terri stood by Gwen the entire time, saying nothing. She glared at the two women berating Gwen.

When the women took notice of Teri, they quickly withdrew and quickly walked away.

Gwen saw the supervisor lean her head in from around the corner.

"It's nothing! It's nothing!"

She turned around and saw Terri walking out the door.

A female hand knocked on the door, just underneath the metal sign.

The top slot of the sign read "WARDEN," but the bottom slot was empty.

Just before she knocked again, she heard the sound of the telephone ring behind the door. A moment later, the sound of a man's voice identified himself to the caller.

The female guard slowly turned the knob and pushed the door open. She saw the middle-aged man with a head full of gray hairs sitting in a big chair, hunched over the desk.

The man heard the creak of his office door and looked up. When seeing one of his guards, he waved for her to come in as he adjusted the phone to his ear.

"Yes, this is the warden. How can I help you? Yes… oh, yes, I was expecting your call. Yes, I have a few minutes…."

*** *** ***

On the other end of the line, in an office in Charleston, three young volunteer lawyers sat around a phone with an intercom. A tall, slender woman dressed in a blue polyester blazer with a baby blue shirt underneath. Across from her was another woman, about a foot shorter. She wore a white short-sleeve shirt and a gray skirt. Next to her was a gentleman about the same height with thick, black horn-rimmed glasses.

The tall woman leaned over the phone system.

"Warden…"

"Nestor!"

"Excuse me," she said, "Warden Nestor, my name is Celeste Petersen. I'm here with my co-workers, Robert Jefferson and Myrtle Gladstone. We were contacted several weeks ago about an incident that occurred at your facility. Several people were injured and we sent for treatment out of your jurisdiction. A couple of them were sent, not to the local hospital but to an institution for the insane. That seems odd to us. After we were alerted to their location, upon consultation with our clients, we believe their civil rights were violated. But, we'd like to hear from you about this incident to get to the bottom of this issue.

"Yes, yes, I know who you are. I've heard of your service to the community and I appreciate you coming all the way over here to help us figure out how we can improve serving our small community here at Pence Springs!"

"Well, yes and no, warden. We're calling, primarily, to first check on the welfare of two of our clients and secondly we'd like to hear your take on how the women were brutalized for an infraction that was largely the result of the neglect of one of your officers."

"Well… I'm sorry… Miss…"

"Petersen."

"Yes, Miss Petersen! I'm afraid that I can only offer you the records from the previous warden…. Blankenship… who retired just a couple of weeks ago. The incident that you're no doubt alluding to happened under her watch. But, what I can tell you is that we had a case where the women — we don't like to call them inmates unless their attitudes dictate as such— but one of the inmates apparently went into a restricted area and stole some personal items from one of the guards. Because the guard violated one of the rules about bringing personal items past the check-in point, we had to reprimand her. It was told to Blankenship, who was off-duty at the time that some of the women, including a…. Gwen… Collins… had refused to stay in the livingroom until all of the women had been investigated and cleared."

"Warden Nestor," Attorney Gladstone said, "We read a copy of the Incident Report from the court in Charleston. But, I'm a bit loss as to why would the staff subject all of the women to a strip search for an amount less than twenty dollars? Can they spend it in there?"

"No, they can't but we still expect the women to follow orders no matter if they like it or not. This is a minimum-security prison, but it's still a prison."

"The state police could have killed any one of those women," Petersen said.

"And, may I add," Jefferson chimed in, "I personally met with Miss Collins on two different occasions before your staff whisked her and Buffy away before we could file an injunction against Blankenship for false imprisonment and excessive force. Did you see the fracture that Miss Collins had? The other inmate… I forgot her legal name, but she told us her nickname is Buffy… had almost all of her hair pulled out? Doesn't that sound excessive to you? Endanger the lives of these women for just twenty dollars?"

"Excuse me, Attorney Jefferson, but I will not have you question the authority of this institution as if we are subject to your jurisdiction. Now I made myself clear to all of you that we attempted to restore order. It was Miss Collins and a few others went to their rooms only after being threatening with an extended sentence but later felt justified in defying the orders of the shift supervisor by coming back down stairs and refusing to move. It was also Gwen Collins who picked up the poker and wielded it so that it brought us to that point."

*** *** ***

"What's the matter Gwen," Mrs. Huffman said as she stood above her at the lunch table.

Gwen looked up with tears streaming down her face. She instinctively pulled the pages of a long letter closer to her. Her face shook a bit in disbelief as she looked back at the letters she received from her great-aunt. This was the same long letter that she started reading the morning before the riot. She took a napkin and wiped her nose.

"My great-aunt wrote me and told me something about one of my sisters. And, no everything is not all right. I got to get outta here, I have to see my sisters and my brothers and my mother."

Mrs. Huffman softly put her hand on Gwen's shoulder, "Gwen, we're working on—" There was a sound a few tables away. Mrs. Huffman turned to the side and noticed the table in a far corner where one tall woman with a closely shaved haircut, oversized shirt, baggy jeans was smoking a cigarette and talking with two women who sat directly across from her.

Another woman, small framed with her hair pulled back into a pony tail, was walking with a tray of food in the direction of Leona.

Leona flicked the cigarette depositing the ashes on the floor behind her.

Mrs. Huffman had taken notice of Camille in times past and wanted to see how she was going to negotiate the small space between Leona's chair and the chairs directly behind her. Mrs. Huffman wasn't surprised to see Camille hold the tray over her head while tippy-toeing very slowly behind Leona.

Whether it was passing Camille in the hallway, room check or getting a glimpse of her during Camille's work duty hours, Mrs. Huffman found it strange that Leona was never more than three feet away from her.

"Hurry up and sit down, don't like nobody standing behind me. Y'hear?" Leona said to Camille but not turning around to say it to her face.

Leona pulled her chair in closer to the table just a little, perhaps offering some sort of diplomacy in the moment. It was then that she turned and noticed Mrs. Huffman watching the exchange. She gave Mrs. Huffman a glare. A glare that Mrs. Huffman had experienced quite a few times in passing.

"Mrs. Huffman… Mrs. Huffman… excuse me!"

Mrs. Huffman turned and saw another guard standing next to her.

"Yes!"

"Mrs. Huffman, the warden wants to see Collins in his office immediately."

Mrs. Huffman turned back to Gwen. "Oh, Gwen! I'm so, so sorry. I don't know what came over me!"

Gwen looked at her while she compiled the papers in front of her. "It's okay. We can talk about it some other time. I'm gonna see what the warden wants."

"Okay, we'll talk later. I'll stop by your room before my last shift ends."

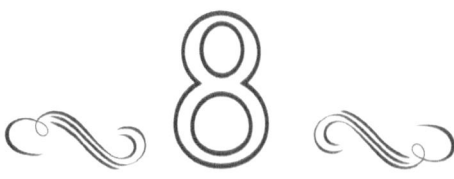

"Let me be clear about one thing. We're not perfect but we try to our best to offer an environment that would help the women to be re-acculturated into their communities. We want them to function as productive citizens."

"That sounds ideal but," Ms. Peterson said, "ideals implemented without proper structure and accountability rarely materialize into reality."

"What we'd like to know, warden, is if you were to put yourself in your predecessor's position for a moment: why were the two women… why were they sent to an insane asylum? What were you trying to hide?"

"Miss Peterson, you seem to overlook the fact that we had an uprising, the safety of our inmates, not to mention that of our staff was and is our primary concern. The previous warden, to our satisfaction followed protocol. The staff, in her absence, carried out their responsibilities as they were trained to. Sure, there's always room for improvement and we regret the accidents that occurred but again, it was a result of their lack of cooperation."

"Warden, we don't want to—"

There was a knock at the door. The warden, who was standing behind his desk and looking out the window, turned when he heard the squeaking sound of the hinges. He saw the door open and Gwen walked through the door that the guard was holding open.

The warden quickly pushed a button silencing the loudspeaker while lifting up the receiver at the same time. He put his hand over the receiver, while looking at Gwen pointed to an empty seat in front of his desk. In a low voice, he whispered, "Please, Miss Collins, have a seat. I'll be with you in a minute."

"I'm sorry, Miss Peterson, I missed the last thing you said."

"Warden, we don't want to belabor the point. What we want to know is what do you have in place that will ensure that there isn't another instance of your institution violating your inmates' rights?"

"We've made substantial changes to our response and we constantly have refresher training periods for our guards according to the state's incarceration guidelines. Yes… I can assure you that we will look at the matter differently if it ever should occur again."

"Perhaps, we can pay a visit to Miss Collins and the woman whose nickname is Buffy from time to time?"

"That would be fine. But, please let us know ahead of time and we'll make arrangements for you."

"Thank you for your time, warden. We'll be in contact."

"Thank you, Miss Peterson." The warden hung up the phone and looked at Gwen. He took a sip of water that was next to the phone, then took a deep breath.

Mrs. Huffman stood at the top of the stairs. Before resuming her rounds, she looked down to the lobby in front of the warden's door, where Gwen and the guard were waiting. She smiled back at Gwen after Gwen turned around. She watched as Gwen walked into the warden's office and the guard followed right after her.

Mrs. Huffman turned and walked down the corridor, checking a box on the clipboard in front of the door that a voice responded to, but her mind was on Gwen and how could she make it through her prison sentence without conflict. It was a puzzling thought and one that she was unsure of. She knew she'd have to keep an eye on her.

A few steps away from the last room on the floor, she heard a voice: a strong but tempered voice coming from the doorway. She knew Leona's voice but she stopped just before the open door to hear some more.

"Now, I done toll you befo', this ain't how I like my pants folded. This ain't where I want my boots leff. Put 'em where I toll you. Oh, and anotha thing, I toll you I want 'cha little narrow ass right beside me at the lunch table.. Where the hell were you?"

Mrs. Huffman leaned in slowly and saw Leona grab Camille by the jaw. Camille was a short, dark-skinned woman of maybe twenty. She kept her arms to the side as Leona raised her face by the grip Leona had on her. Mrs. Huffman saw the fear in her eyes and Camille's short permed hair which was pulled tightly to the back fell out of the small rubber band which held it.

"I… I…had to go to the bathroom. I had to pee," Camille struggled to say with her mouth contorted.

Seeing this, Mrs. Huffman stamped her foot in the doorway.

"LADIES… ROOM CHECK!"

Leona turned around suddenly, dropping her hands behind her and walking briskly to Mrs. Huffman. "Yeah, we here! Can't you see that or do you like hearing our voices?"

"I don't hear both of you, just yours." Mrs. Huffman took her eyes off Leona and looked behind her, seeing a small-framed woman shaking by the bed. "Camille, are you alright?"

Camille nodded in silence.

"Are you sure? You don't have to be afraid, I'm right here."

"She said, she's all right. Now, what mo' do you want from her?"

Mrs. Huffman and Leona stared at each other for a second. "I'm watching you, Leona! I'm watching! Lights out in thirty minutes. And, I better not hear any noise coming from this room."

Leona stood there stone faced as Mrs. Huffman walked out the door.

Mrs. Huffman took a few steps, then took a few notes as she glanced back at the room. She walked a few more feet and looked into a quiet room. A quiet room that she almost thought was empty until a woman sitting on a chair rocking back and forth and knitting came into her peripheral vision.

"Vonda?"

"Present," a voice said.

"Vonda!"

"Yes, ma'am. I'm here."

"Is everything alright?"

"Yes, ma'am. Everything's alright."

Mrs. Huffman was about to leave when she turned to Vonda, who was still slowly rocking and knitting in silence.

"Vonda, may I ask you a question?"

"Yes, ma'am. Go ahead."

"Why are you here? You don't seem like a person who'd commit a crime?"

"No, ma'am. I did commit a crime. I killed my husband."

"Oh… my god."

"Wanna know why?"

Mrs. Huffman nodded.

"I killed my husband because he was so mean to me. He treated me so bad. He used to beat me and beat me. He beat me for everything you could think of. When it wasn't this, it was that. When he had a bad day at work, he used to come home and take it out on me. And, sometimes when he'd go out on the weekends to the bar with some of the neighbors, he'd bring them back here and tell them to come see me in our bedroom."

"WHAT!"

"Yes. And, I had to sleep with all of them. Mostly, one at a time but sometimes with two of them at the same time. And, I had to do whatever they wanted me to do. I couldn't say, no."

"Vonda… no…"

"Mrs. Huffman, my husband was an evil man. I don't know why except I do know he had a drinking problem and a gambling problem. So right there, I figured they were having me to pay off his debts."

"So…"

"So, one Sunday morning, I got up and instead of making his breakfast, I waited outside on the porch with his gun. I sat right there on the rocking chair waiting for him to come outside cussin' about his breakfast. He did. I knew he would and I shot him right there. Then, I shot him again. I couldn't take it anymore. I dragged his body over to where we grilled the hogs. Then I chopped him up, burnt him and buried the rest."

"Oh, dear Lord, Vonda!"

"I know, Mrs. Huffman, it sounds terrible but it was either him or me. And, I ain't done nothing to deserve him treatin' me like that."

Mrs. Huffman nodded then said, "Goodnight, Vonda. Lights out in about… twentyfive minutes. Okay?"

Vonda said nothing but went back to rocking in her chair and resumed her knitting.

Mrs. Huffman slowly walked out into the corridor with her clipboard in hand and keys dangling from her waist. She stopped and leaned her body against the wall. She took a couple of deep breaths, then resumed her walk back to the stairs.

"Miss Collins," Warden Nestor said, as he fixed his wire-framed glasses, "I want to ask you a favor, if you don't mind. Do you want to make a deal with me?"

"Yes… sir? What kind of deal are we talking about?"

"Miss Collins, we don't like trouble. Trouble is good for no one. Trouble only causes more trouble. So what I'm saying is…can you find a way to stay out of trouble? I mean, if someone bothers you…if someone wants to provoke you into some kind of altercation, can you just walk away or at the very least, ignore it?"

"Yes, sir."

He exhaled. "This is what I'm going to do. I'm going to pretend as if these little matters with you and some of the other inmates had never happened. That's it. It never happened. It…or should I say, they disappeared from my books. Do you know what that means?"

"Not quite, but I'm listening."

"Miss Collins, I can see that you have a parole hearing coming up in a few short weeks. If there's nothing to report since your last infraction, then there's a good possibility that you could make parole."

Gwen's eyes lit up. "That's it? Just stay out of trouble?"

"That's it. But, I need you to do me a favor." Tipping down his glasses, "I need you to let our… our little misunderstandings go. There's no need to bring the matter up again. No good can come from that. Do I make myself clear?"

"Forgotten. Yeah, I think I can do that. I just want to go home and see my little girl."

West sat upright in his seat but with every wide turn and every bump in the road, he slid out of place. It aggravated him because he had to push his injured leg to move the crutches closer to his free hand to be picked up.

He looked out of the window of the school and saw the traffic getting heavier as it approached his high school. He saw some students walking briskly with new knapsacks and sneakers. Guys chasing each other in the courtyard and girls hugging and laughing with each other. West also saw some familiar faces on the basketball team waving to him from afar. He took a deep breath and thought about how he'd manage on this first day of school.

The bus came to as sudden stop and the students in front of West filled the line to disembark. He was fortunate to have a few friends around him who were patient to help him up, gather his bag and his crutches.

As he made his way down the steps, the crowd in front of him parted and there stood a young woman. She was about five foot two, ninety pounds and her straight, waistlength brunette hair was now shoulder length. More than anything, West recognized her wispy smile.

"I'M BACK," Sandy said as some students behind West was overheard saying, "Awww, West, don't mind that. We know it's been over between you two for awhile. Get out the way!"

"You're back! What do you mean? What are you doing here?"

"I talked my dad into letting me come back. What happened to you?"

West carefully made the last few steps off the bus, when Sandy grabbed his knapsack off his shoulder. He looked at her for a second, looked around, then leaned in for a kiss. They talked as if no one else in that crowded field was around until they both disappeared through the front door of the school.

*** *** ***

It was a dizzying time for West. School had just started. It was just weeks before that West pulled some ligaments in his right leg. He was in a local band, accepted to play on the school's basketball and track teams. And, there were the girlfriends that West made being a letterman. Now, Sandy was back in the picture. How was he going to manage so many affairs? Could he juggle all of those balls in the air or was he going to lose his balance? One thing West was certain of, he had no place to hide.

*** *** ***

"Okay, now, I want you boys to say grace before you eat. We respect the Lord in this house. Now, Petey, why don't you say grace this time since West did it last week?"

"Awww, Auntie Minerva, I ain't no religious guy. The Lord knows I'm thankful cause I'm gonna eat everything on this plate."

"Aunt Minerva?"

"Yes, Jeff" Minerva said, a bit taken by surprise. "Do you have enough to eat?"

"Yes, ma'am. I just wanted to thank you again for the breakfast. This is like a full course meal at my house. Mom doesn't cook pancakes and biscuits with gravy and eggs and potatoes at the same meal. I could say grace, if you want me to?"

Minerva dried her hands on the small towel that hung from her apron, then looked at Petey and West. "You see! This young man comes from a good family. It don't take a whole lot to be grateful. Jeff, you just said grace and I want to thank you."

"Now, Petey, and West, I want you two to take care of the dishes and the pots when you're finished. I'm going in the back to hang the rest of those clothes."

"Yes, Auntie," West said as he smiled at Petey.

A couple of minute passed when the sound of forks hitting ceramic plates was interrupted by the sound of the phone. Petey was about to reach for it when West pulled him back.

"Will somebody get the phone" was heard coming from the backyard as the phone rang a second time.

West spoke in a low voice, "Wait, if it stops after the third time, then it's for me. Let's just wait. I'll fill you in later."

After the third time, the phone became silent. West crept to the phone and motioned for Petey and Jeff to continue eating. He turned back and dialed a number and cupped the receiver.

"Hello… Sandy… yeah, I can't talk long. I got people over. Yeah, I wanna see you too. You're all I think about. I think about you when I go to bed, when I wake up. I even think about you when I'm in class. You're the reason why I'm failing math!"

"West," Petey called out in a low voice, "who is that you talkin' to?"

"Shhhh," West said as he turned to him, "go on and finish. I'll be with you in a minute." West turned around and stood on the other side of the wall. "Sandy, I hate it as much as you do, but I can't come over to your house, you know how your dad feels about me! I'll tell you what. I gotta plan! Leave it up to me and I promise you we'll have a lot more time together. Okay? Great! I'll call you later tonight… okay, bye… okay, I love you, too!"

West hung up the phone but before he could get back to the kitchen table, Minerva was standing in front of him with an arm full of folded clothes.

"I see you have time to talk sweet nothings to that girl but you won't volunteer to say grace. West, Jr., you better leave that white girl alone before those white folks hang you."

"No, Auntie, it ain't that way! We're just friends. We're talking about doing homework after school some time."

Minerva looked at him her head tilted back.

"Auntie, I'll take care of the dishes when I get back. Me and Petey and Jeff have to go somewhere to pick up something for Mr. Walker. Ain't that right, Jeff?"

Jeff looked up startled, "Yeah! We gotta pick something up for my dad. Thanks for breakfast, Aunt Minerva. We'll be back soon."

Aunt Minerva had her arms crossed as squeaky sound of the front door's hinges echoed in the kitchen.

Some weeks went by, then a few months. Pence looked different to Gwen. It looked awkward. Some of the people who sat at certain tables weren't there one day, then another and another. Soon, areas that belonged to certain people became vacant. New residents came in and Pence seemed like a totally new place.

But one thing remained the same, Gwen was alone doing her time. No more Charleston girls, no more card games. Her empty room seemed like the only safe place for her to retreat.

As she walked up the stairs after breakfast, she heard her name called.

"Collins… Collins. Can we see you for a few minutes?"

Gwen turned around and noticed a guard holding a letter in her hand.

"Collins, the warden would like to talk with you. He also told me to give this to you."

When Gwen came to the room, she was met by the warden and another officer, an older female officer who sat directly across from Warden Nestor. She looked a little like Blankenship except she seemed to be a bit bigger in the torso and her hair was totally white with a couple of faint streaks of yellow. She also had a pair of reading glasses attached to a chain that hung around her neck. She looked up to Gwen and nodded but didn't say anything.

"Miss Collins," Nestor said, "Please have the other seat. This is Mrs. Parker. She works with the parole board. She helps inmates to find sponsors so that they can be released and become reacquainted with society once they leave our facility.

"I asked Mrs. Parker if she could come this morning to speak with you because from our last conversation, you mentioned that you didn't have anyone on the outside whom could help you if you won parole.

"Now, I've been monitoring your progress since we last spoke and I'm satisfied with your progress and since you've had no infringements for some time, I think we can proceed with this line of discussion. I'm a man of my word. The letter you are holding is for your upcoming parole hearing on Wednesday…. yes, Wednesday. So, you'll need to prepare yourself for that. I've already signed off on this meeting."

Gwen's eyes sparkled with excitement. "Does this mean that I'm being paroled?"

"No, not exactly. It means that you have nothing blocking you except the answers you give to their questions. My advice to you is to think about what you've learned by being here. What were the decisions you made to bring you here and what will change if you're given another chance. The parole board is looking for repentance and contrition. In other words, do you know what you did wrong, do you accept responsibility for actions and how will things be different from now on.

"I wanted Mrs. Parker to help you find someone in the community to vouch for you until your probationary period has elapsed. So, Mrs. Parker will take it from here."

Gwen and Mrs. Parker faced each other, with Gwen confirming the information about her family, work history and health. All the while, Mrs. Parker was taking notes on a small pad. She opened a folder, thumbing through some resumes until she pulled one out.

"Gwen, I've spoken with a couple of families about you since the warden called. I wanted to line a few up with the hopes that you'll finally make parole. I'd like to place you with a family that lives in Princeton. Have you ever been to Princeton?"

"Yes, Mrs. Parker. We drove through there once."

"This is a nice family and they're known to take in people who don't have anywhere to go. They're an older couple with two adult children, a couple of grandchildren and a few placements. Do you think you can manage in this environment?"

"I guess. I don't know."

"I'll need an answer or I'll have to wait until there's a more suitable arrangement. Perhaps, you might want to call your mother in Kentucky and have her to take you back?"

"No, ma'am! No! I don't want to move back. I'll make it work with the family. If they'd have me. I just need a chance. That's all I need."

Mrs. Parker looked at Gwen for a moment, then looked at the warden who nodded in agreement. "Okay, then it's settled. If they approve your release, they'll ask you if you have a sponsor, you'll tell them yes and it's been confirmed."

Mrs. Parker stood up and extended her hand to Gwen. "Gwen,

I've heard a lot of good things about you. I hope things work out for you. The warden is very proud of you as well. We're hoping the best for you in the future."

Gwen nodded with a smile.

"Miss Collins," the warden interrupted, "I need to finish a conversation I was having with Mrs. Parker. You can leave now. Please prepare yourself for the parole board and good luck."

"Thank you, sir." Gwen turned and walked slowly out of the room, smiling.

Two days went by like two hours, but the hours before the meeting seemed to drag.

Gwen awoke early on Wednesday with an elevated heartbeat and sweaty hands. She walked to the sink and poured water over her head and face. The weight of the meeting with the parole board felt heavier than ever before. This time, she felt, she really had a chance but she feared not saying the right thing. All she had were the questions Warden Nestor gave her to consider.

When the knock on her door finally happened, she stood up, took a deep breath and wiped her sweaty hands on her dress.

She sat on the opposite side of the long table facing three people that seemed disinterested in her. She kept reminding herself to see herself out of Pence and to be holding her child.

Gwen answered the first few questions about her identity and the charges that originally sent her to Pence. Each time, noticing the three judges writing down notes on a large pad in front of each of them.

Then the lone man who sat directly in front of Gwen spoke up.

"Miss Collins, we've been through this before. In fact, we've been through this several times before. What makes this time any different than before? What can you tell us to make you believe that you're a changed person?"

Gwen looked at her shaky hands that were resting on her lap.

"I've learned a lot since I've been here. In the past couple of months I realized that I'm the reason why I'm here. No one else. I chose to keep company with the wrong crowd. I chose to do drugs with my boyfriend. I am guilty of the crimes I was convicted of. I have no one to blame for my life but me. "But, I also came to the conclusion that I can do better, if you give me a chance. I want the chance to go back to school. I want the chance to be a mother to my daughter. I want the chance to be a part of the good community… the kind that my great grandmother and my Nanna help to build. I know I can be. I went in the wrong direction, but being here has showed me that I didn't need to take shortcuts to make it.

"If you give me a chance, I can prove to myself and I can show you that I'm a changed person. I just need one chance. I promise, I won't let you down."

"Miss Collins," the lady on the left said, "If we grant you parole, you'd need a place to go and you need to have a plan for your future. Do you have these requirements worked out?"

"Yes, ma'am. I'd move in with a family named, The Strains. They're a good family and they know all about me and they believe in me. As far as my plans are concerned, I plan to get a job immediately. I'm going to save up and hope to be fully independent within one year. From there, I plan to enroll in college a year after that."

The three moderators looked at each other, then wrote down some more notes. The woman on the right looked at Gwen.

"Miss Collins, there are a few things we'd like to discuss amongst ourselves, check the reports given to us before we make a final call. Could you please wait outside? I think we'll be able to give you an answer in a few minutes."

Gwen paced back and forth in front of the conference room door. She replayed the moments in that room in her mind, minute by minute. She thought about the questions. She tried to extrapolate what their expressions meant; the length of time and the notes they took. Nothing she thought about gave her any inclination as to how they were going to act. She resolved to think about the warden's promise, the work of Mrs. Parker. She also thought about her friend, Mrs. Huffman and the many prayers they made together. It's got to work out this time, she thought.

"Miss Collins!"

Gwen opened her eyes. "Miss Collins, you can come in now."

Gwen slowly walked in the door, but this time all three of the moderators were standing with all of their notepads neatly tucked away in manilla folders in front of them. Their pens were capped and the glasses of water were completely empty.

"Miss Collins," the gentleman said, "we all agree that you have showed vast improvements in your demeanor. You've accepted total responsibility and blamed no one for your mistakes. You seem focused and are ready to live a better life. Therefore, we are please to approve your parole. We have signed off on your release to the Strains and we wanted to wish you good luck in your new life."

Gwen, stunned, walked over to each of them and thanked them.

To each of them she whispered, "I won't let you let down."

Gwen walked slowly down the stairs balancing her bags with every step she took. She was also balancing the excitement of leaving Pence with the fear of what was next. She saw two older people sitting on chairs adjacent to the main office window. After she made eye-contact, Mr. Strain, a short, balding and bespeckled man in his early 60's, mouthed the words, Do you need help? The woman who sat beside him, momentarily distracted by guards walking in an out of the dining room saw Gwen struggling with her bags, nudged him, "George, go help her! What'chu sittin' here for?" "COLLINS!"

"Yes..." She said, as she turned in the direction of the voice.

One of the guards was holding the shoe box that Gwen kept all of the letters and a couple of loose cigarettes. "You forgot this in the room It looks important."

"Oh, my gosh! Thank you! Oh my god, thank you! Thank you" "You're welcome. Well...good luck. I wish you much... Gwen... I hope you find happiness. Just do me a favor?" "Sure, what is it?" "When you walk out the door, don't look back."

"Oh, I won't! Trust me, I'm never coming back!"

The guard shook her head slowly, "Never say never and... and whatever you do, don't look back until after you leave our gates."

Mr. Strain took one of Gwen's bags as Orangie opened the back door of the 4-door sedan. From a distance, Gwen heard her named called, followed by the words, goodbye! Gwen turned from stepping in the car and turned around to see who was calling her but seeing no one. She raised her hand to block the rays from early morning sun but not seeing anyone, she screamed out, "Good bye!"

Orangie and George didn't look at each other as they left. George took the wheel and Orangie talked with Gwen without ever looking back at her.

*** *** ***

Princeton was like all of the other small towns in West Virginia; small houses, vacant lots, unkempt shrubs and the occasional strip mall. Several things crossed Gwen's mind as she peered through the car window. How could she live in a place that had no life and how could she start over having nothing but what was in her bags. It was then that she realized that her time in Charleston was all in vain. She had absolutely nothing to show for the time she invested there.

The car pulled up in front of a small white house. The faded blue curtains in the front room shook before settling.

"Don't mind them, Gwen. They like to get up into things they shouldn't," Orangie said. "I set a place for you downstairs, so you can have your privacy. George…George!"

"Yes, dear!"

"George, did you remember to put Xavier's stuff by the stairs?"
"Yes, dear."

"Okay, Gwen, I'm gonna introduce you to everyone after you get settled in but I'm gonna set out a plate for you at the table."

"Thank you, ma'am," Gwen stared at the house, then turned around in a circle looking at the neighborhood. She looked to the sky and exhaled. She silently prayed that her luck would change.

It had been a couple of weeks since Gwen moved into the Strains' home. Still, she felt a bit uneasy being in the home of people she barely knew. It was a struggle getting out of bed each morning. She didn't know whom she was going to meet upstairs for breakfast. Was it the friendly, talkative Orangie who seemed both protective and mothering? Or, was it the sarcastic Orangie who stood over you without saying a word?

Gwen sat at the table across from the three kids the Strains were baby sitting. They wouldn't sit still and were always getting into some kind of mischief. It wasn't unusual to see them hide pieces of clothing from Orangie or George, causing them to blame each other for being absentminded.

Before she made it to the steps, she noticed a duffle bag along with some boxes that were in a pile adjacent to the stairs. It had been there since she moved in, but she struggled with the temptation to open the bag to see what was in it. The only deterrent being a vague comment she remembered Mr. Strain mentioned about somebody supposedly coming by to pick them up. She just didn't remember whom.

She put the last teaspoon of cereal in her mouth when she heard Orangie, in a loud voice, in the living room wondering where her pills were.

"Where are my pills? Has anyone seen my pills! I couldn't have misplaced my pills! There always right there on my nightstand!

George! George, are you sure you didn't move my pills?"

George grumbled something unintelligible that made Orangie walk away in disgust. She walked to the kitchen and threw the dish towel she had on the space next to Gwen's plate, while she readjusted her apron. Slowly she looked up at Gwen: "Well," Orangie said a high, nasal-tone, "We never had anyone come into our home and steal from us. Ain't that right, George? George....George... are you listening to me?"

Gwen heard a newspaper crinkle, then the sound of a faint murmur of agreement. "George, you ain't no help! No help, whatsoever!" Orangie wiped her hands on her apron and walked to the stove, "You know, I think it's about time that we get everyone who's of age to get a job. It's expensive feeding all these grown folks. We can't have freeloaders here, you know money don't grow on trees."

Orangie walked back to the table and briefly watched the kids play finger football with a green pea, then looked silently stared at Gwen.

Gwen looked at Orangie as she stood in the kitchen doorway looking out to the livingroom. Nothing needed to be said. Gwen knew she couldn't get too comfortable because the welcome-mat was surely being pulled away.

*** *** ***

As she walked down the stairs to her room, Gwen had resolved that she wouldn't let Orangie see her intimidated. She vowed Orangie wouldn't get the satisfaction of seeing her cry.

Reaching near the middle of the staircase, she saw someone

bending down at the bottom where the bag and boxes were.

The person stood upright, pulling up the bag to his shoulder. There he stood, all 5'8" of him. Light-skinned with sandy red hair. White tee shirt, blue jeans and Chuck Taylor's on his feet.

He smiled. His clean-shaven face revealed his pearly-white teeth. "Hey, I'm sorry it took so long to get my stuff. I just finished a setup job. You must be Gwen. My grandparents told me all about you. She also told me that I needed to get my stuff out here to make room for you."

"That's okay," Gwen said. "You didn't tell me your name."

"Oh, I'm Xavier!"

"Xavier! That's a nice name." Gwen started down the stairs a little faster as if her momentary reluctance to move was just a distant memory. "You don't have to move your stuff, it's not in my way."

Xavier, who was now less than a foot away, smelled very nice to her. His new shirt fit him perfectly and his after-shave cologne reminded her of the fragrance counter at the department store she visited a few days earlier where she put in an application.

"Do you know of any place hiring? I need a job. I'll do anything."

Xavier looked up to the ceiling, then looked back down, "Well, if you don't mind the long hours, the Dollar store is hiring. You might want to try there?"

"I wish I could. I'm new here and I have no clue where that is."

"It's not far," Xavier said. "In fact, I'll drive you over there now, if you want."

Nothing was going to deter West from being with Sandy. He smiled to himself when he saw Hattie nod to him from her seat near the front of their English class. She folded a piece of paper and when Mrs. Miller turned to write a comment on the blackboard, she reached behind her and passed it to the girl who was reaching out.

The small, wrinkled piece of paper made its way from desk to desk to West's eager hand. He clutched it while standing up the text book from Mrs. Miller's view.

"West," he remembered his Aunt Minerva warning, *"you better leave that girl alone! I don't wanna get a phone call to come and cut you down from a tree!"*

He looked up quickly, peering over the book to see where Mrs. Miller was. He looked down to the opened note:

"West, I'm just thinking about you. I just want you to know that you're my man and I'm your girl. You don't have anything to worry about. I'm right here for you. I don't care what my father thinks, I know what I feel and I know what I want and I want you. I want to be with you every minute of the day. I can't wait to see you after school at our spot! Love, S!"

"WEST WOMACK!"

West looked up to see his English teacher looking down at him. "Yes, ma'am. I'm listening."

"You're listening, huh? What's that you're reading? It sure doesn't look like Mark Twain."

"Oh, no ma'am. I was just looking at... the grocery list my auntie gave me to pick up after school."

Mrs. Miller stared at West for a second, "I won't ask you to hand it to me, but it seems like someone's who's still walking around with a limp aught not to be putting too much weight on it."

"No, ma'am, the stuff is not heavy and my legs are getting better every day."

"Alright now," Mrs. Miller said as she turned back to the class while walking up the aisle, "who is the protagonist in A Connecticut Yankee In King Arthur's Court?"

The bell rang roughly twenty minutes later and the students were running for the door. Mrs. Miller looked at West as she was erasing the board. "West, can you come here for a second?"

"Yes, ma'am?"

"West, you're a good kid. You have a bright future ahead of you. Everybody likes you because you're the class clown and a star athlete but don't let other things get in the way of you getting good grades. If sports don't work out, you'll need the smarts to get a scholarship to pay for college. A college education is something no one can ever take away from you."

"Thank you, ma'am. I won't let you down."

West walked slowly out into the bustling hallway when he saw one of his teammates smiling and calling out his name.

"Hey man, gotta minute?"

"Yeah man, what's happening!"

"Look man, I need a favor from you. You think you can write something for me? I need to make this girl pay attention to me. Jones told me that you charge two dollars for a love letter. You think you can do that for me?"

West looked casually around the crowded hallway. He leaned in closer and spoke in a lower voice, "Yeah, I think I can do something for but you can't approach me like this in front of all these people. I'll tell you what. Because you're my friend, I'll do it for you for two dollars. I only charge my close friends that amount. It's gonna take about a week cause I have to do some research on the subject."

The guy reached into his pocket and pulled out a dollar bill and a few coins. "This is all I got. Can I get the rest to you later?"

"Okay, but I don't usually work on layaway. Just have the rest for me before the game on Thursday. What's her name anyway?"

"Pamela."

"Pamela... you mean the girl with the-"

"Yeah! Yeah!"

"Man, you're something else. All right, I'll get with you later."

West shook hands with his teammate and walked off laughing.

*** *** ***

West opened his eyes and watched as Sandy opened hers. The kiss was a little longer than usual, but he knew by how fast her heart was beating that it was real.

He took a half step back but still held both of her hands in his. "My cherie amour, you're the only one I adore."

"West, I don't know where you come up with these lines." She let go of his hands and hugged him. She looked up at him as she laid her head on his chest, "Tell me, you're the only one for me."

"You know I am. I don't have eyes for any other girl. Why do you think I take so much heat from my family and friends for you? They don't want me to give up on you. They see a different side to me and it's all because of you."

"Oh, West! I dream about us getting married and having a family-"

"Wait! Sandy, what time you got?"

"It's…three forty three. Why?"

"I gotta go! Aunt Minerva is expecting me early today. She was getting home early and she wants me and Petey to have dinner early. Can I walk you home tomorrow?" West quickly kisses her.

"Yeah… sure."

West stepped to the side and saw one of his teammates waiting for the next school bus. He whistled twice, then waved to him to come over.

Sandy tapped West on the shoulder, "What're you doing?"

"It's gonna be alright!"

"West," his teammate said as he jogged in their direction, "what's happening man!"

"Hey, Brian, do me a favor, man. I need you to walk this young lady to her house for me. You think you can do that for me?"

"Well, I was about to-"

West pulled out a dollar and a few coins and put it in his hand, "Are we square?"

"Yeah, man, we're cool."

"But, West," Sandy said, "Wait!"

West was about three yards away. As he continued to run, he looked back, "Sandy, I gotta go. He's a friend. You'll be alright. I'll talk to you tomorrow."

West ran at full speed until he was out of their sight. He walked until he reached the top of the hill which overlooked the area's recreation center. He was out of breath but remembered there was a water-fountain inside the center.

West opened the main door to see a group of women. These were most of the black women who lived in the area. Women of all ages. They were there to have their monthly, *Women's Rap*

Session.

When it was this time, the men in the area knew to stay far, far away because it usually meant the area's dirty laundry was about to be aired and it wasn't going to be pretty.

Older women compared notes with the other older women about their husbands or boyfriends (or, both) and the younger women were there to learn from *their mistakes.*

West didn't think anything of it when he came in. He figured he'd quickly get some water, wave and get out as fast as he could. Today was different. It was meaner than usual. It was darker than usual. And, the expressions on their faces told him, it was nastier than usual.

"There he go! He's another one of them!"

Another voice said, "I knew he was no good ever since his momma dropped him off."

West turned his head from left to right, then pointed to himself.

"Who me? What did I do?"

"Yeah," a third voice screamed out. "He's one of those good-for-nothing's! West Womack, you ain't nuthin but a low-down dirty shame! We seen you with that snowbunny behind the school. You can't hide your shame. What? You too good to talk to one of us. All of a sudden, you too good to talk to one of your own? Those white girls got your head all messed up?"

West walked over to the water fountain and took a sip and slowly walked away. It looked to the group that he was about to leave when he reversed and walked back to the front of the circle.

"I hear y'all always talkin' about this man and that man. And, this man ain't no good. And, that man dresses like this and that man ain't got the looks to be seen out in public with.

"Y'all wanna hear the truth. None of you ain't got no one because of you. Your mouth is too big. You think you're too good for any of the guys around here. You… you over there," West said as he point to a woman in the circle, "when I tried to talk to you, you told me that you don't got time for me. And, you… you told me to go on and get outta here because I don't own a car. And, you… you over there, I see you. You told me that I'm too young for you and that you only date older guys.

"Now that those guys, those older guys, those guys with money and a car, got what they wanted and left you, you think all men are dogs.

"So, what I'm supposed to do? Since none of you wanted to date me, I asked the white girls out. They said, yes! They don't care that I don't have a lot of money. They don't care that I don't wear expensive clothes. All they want is for us to be nice to them.

"So, y'all can talk mess all you want! Y'all didn't want me when I was single and now that you ain't got someone, you wanna blame guys like me." West adjusted his backpack on his shoulder and started to walk to the door, "Y'all can be miserable all you want, when you had me, you should have been nice to me. I'm gone and I ain't turning back."

The door slammed behind West and not one voice was heard.

17

Her head jerked from side to side and with each turn, she mumbled. The three kids were wondering who Gwen was talking to.

They tiptoed around her bed and placed a feather at the tip of her nose, running away at the thought of her opening her eyes.

This went on for a couple of minutes before a burly woman crouched down on the stairs, "Jelisa, Styme and Merrick! Leave her alone! Come on, get upstairs before your breakfast gets cold," Orangie said as she peered past them to see Gwen slowly pulling herself up. "And, you, Sleeping Beauty… You… Your PO is upstairs waiting to talk to you. Don't keep him waiting, he's a busy man."

Gwen closed her eyes, took a deep breath as the creaking sound of the steps underneath Orangie's feet disappeared behind the door leading to the living room.

A few minutes passed when Gwen walked through the door to see her parole officer sitting on the living room couch talking with Orangie. It was Thursday and Thursdays were Orangie's beauty shop appointment day. She never missed them. Orangie looked back at Gwen when she noticed, the parole officer's attention was distracted to something behind her.

Orangie gave Gwen one last glance and wedged her big, black handbag underneath her arm. She walked out the front door without saying a word to anyone.

"Gwen, it's good to see you. How're things going?" Mr. Jones said as he stood up and extended his hand.

Gwen cleared her throat. "Good. Everything's fine."

"Well, I was in the neighborhood, so I decided to stop by and see how you were doing."

"Okay?"

"Well… Why don't we come over here and sit down for a few minutes." He looked over to George, who was still sitting some feet away with the newspaper up to his head. "Sir… Mister… Strain?"

"Oh, yes sir."

"Is it alright with you that we talk for a moment? We'll just be a few minutes."

"Oh! Oh, that all right. I'll just sit outside there on the porch. Take your time."

As soon as George walked outside, Mr. Jones turned to Gwen. "I want to be honest with you: I was called by Mrs. Strain. She had some complaints about you and I wanted to find out from you if there's a problem here."

"No, sir. Nothing that I can think."

"Well, Mrs. Strain…Orangie…feels as if you've been disrespectful toward her family. She says that you don't speak to her or George and you won't help around the house." He flipped through his small notepad. "She said, you lounge around the house all day and won't go out to look for work. She spoke to my supervisor the day I was off and told her that she suspected you of stealing her medications."

"Oh, my god! Oh, my god! That's such a lie! I didn't do anything to her. I didn't steal anything from her. I don't know where she's getting that information from."

"I say good morning to everyone. When I come upstairs, she's the one who has an attitude. Some days, she'll say good morning. Some days she'll grumble to herself and throw a plate on the table. Sometimes, I don't even eat breakfast here, I'll go over to Aunt Gaye to eat."

"What! Who…Who's Aunt Gaye?" "

Aunt Gaye lives right there behind us in her trailer. She's Mrs. Strain's sister."

"Oh, okay. So, she lives on the property."

"Yes. And, it's these kids who steal or hide and throw away her pills. That's not me."

"Did you tell her that?"

"I told her but she thinks they're angels. She'd always say, what are they gonna do with my pills?"

"I see." Mr. Jones, hearing the sound of the kids playing in the kitchen, looked sullen for a moment. "I can try to find you a different place but it may mean that you'll have to go back to Pence. You only have three months left until your parole is up.

Do you think you can stick it out until then?"

"Three months?"

'Three months. Then, you'll be legally free to walk away from here without having to report to the state but it'll mean that you'll have to swallow your pride or maybe bite your tongue until then. Do you think you can handle it?"

She thought for a moment. Taking a deep breath, "Yes, I can."

"Good!" Mr. Jones took a deep breath. "I'm going to put down in my report that there was nothing unusual and that the sponsors have too much responsibilities for children far too young for her and her husband to handle."

Looking at her, "Gwen, I can't be anymore clear than this: You must stay out of trouble. Avoid confrontations and whatever you do, try to find a job and save some money to rent a place because you'll be on your own sooner rather than later. Am I making myself clear?"

"Perfectly."

"Great. I'm going to say say goodbye to Mr. Strain but if you need anything, please call."

Gwen decided against eating breakfast, instead the talk of Aunt Gaye gave Gwen the inspiration of eating lunch with her. After her shower, she got dressed, taking a scrap of paper with the names and numbers of stores in the area to call. She came upstairs and opened the door leading to the living room, however, glancing through the living room window, she noticed Aunt Gaye leaving. She stomped her foot in frustration.

With nowhere to go, she slid off her shoes and sat on the couch. She got up and turned on the tv that was directly across from the couch. There wasn't anything of interest playing, she just wanted something on to keep her company.

She started to watch a soap opera when one of the guys reminded her of Xavier. She smiled as she began to feel sleepy. The couch wasn't broad and she found herself turning every once in a while to feel comfortable.

She had realized it but she had dozed off when she felt someone touching her. She was startled but knew it could only be George. She knew he was leaning over her. She was terrified, wanting and needing him to stop, she did the only thing she could think of in that second: couch and yawn.

She twisted her body and outstretched her hands and when she felt him leaving, she knew the worse was over. He was kneeling beside the couch, holding her wrist against the couch and with his free hand, touching her breasts.

He said nothing but stood up and walked over to the his recliner that was a few feet away and began to read the paper again.

Gwen's heart rate raced as she stayed still for a few moments. She thought about who to tell and what were the consequences. She thought about Orangie. She thought about how that conversation would play out. S he thought about Mr. Jones and the precautions he gave. She thought about her living situation and the distinct possibility of being sent back to Pence with her parole being violated.

She wanted to look around to see where he was but was afraid to make eye contact with him. She coughed. Then she coughed again.

Mr. Strain ruffled the newspaper and Gwen took that as her cue to get up and leave.

She softly walked downstairs to her room. Once she was inside of the door, she ran to her bed.

She cried.

18

"Are you gonna tell me what's wrong, or am I supposed to guess?" Xavier took a hit of the joint, he just lit up. He held the vapor in for a second with his eyes closed, then he took another long drag before passing it on to Gwen.

She looked around especially focusing in on the window just above them. She wanted to make sure that Orangie wasn't peering out of it. She took a long, deliberate inhale and held it in her cheeks while turning the joint around and around between her index and thumb. She closed her eyes then gently released it in the air as she passed the weed back to Xavier.

"You know, I wish I could move someplace where people didn't know me. I could just change my name and start all over again. Sometimes, I wish I could just be somebody's else. Anybody! I don't care. I just need a break."

"Well," Xavier said through the billow of gray smoke in front of his face, "that ain't happenin'. You gotta put your best foot forward. We're here to help you."

"We who? I know you ain't talking about your grandparents cause Orangie hates me and she wants me out!"

"Grandma doesn't hate you. She just doesn't know you."

"That's easy for you to say. You can't see what I see because of the money and presents she always gives you. I gotta get my own place and I gotta get outta here as soon as possible."

"What about the application at the dollar store?"

Gwen looked at him and smiled as she received the joint back. "I think I got it!"

"Yeah? How do you know?"

"Listen! I passed the polygraph test! My ex- Jink taught me how to do this tapping thing with my feet and he told me what to think about when they would ask the questions and that was it."

Xavier scratched his head in disbelief. "Well, when are you gonna know if you got the job?"

"I'm supposed to call back this lady this afternoon about four. The man who gave me the application told me that if I got the job that I'd have to come in fill out some more papers and maybe starting training that afternoon."

"That's great but you still want to leave even with a job?"

"I'm gonna lose my mind if I stay here too long."

Xavier shook his head slowly, "Come over here!" He walked to the side of the house away from the kitchen window and stood by the wall.

Gwen took another drag and followed him to the spot.

Xavier took the joint from her and placed her arms on top of his shoulders. "You listen to me and you listen good. You're my lady now and I'm gonna look after you. If you're not happy, I'm not happy. I don't care about what happened in the past. The past ain't where I'm headed. It ain't where we're headed. We're gonna find a place where we can live together. You got me?"

"Yeah, I got you." Then she looked down to see his hands grasping her waist. She looked up and found Xavier's lips pressed against hers.

Some weeks went by and Gwen had settled into her work routine at the dollar-store. She winced when told the position only paid the minimum wage of two dollars and sixty-five cents an hour. She concluded that something earned and saved meant something towards her moving expenses. The thought of moving out of Orangie and George's house exhilarated her.

She was stocking the shelves when a young woman, maybe around twenty-five, stopped her to inquire about laundry detergent. Gwen commented on her earrings and they developed a rapport that continued every time this woman, named Lucille, came to the store.

One afternoon, when Gwen was at the cash register, she looked up and saw Lucille at the back of the back of the line. It was also about the time that Gwen was supposed to clock out. Thinking about the ride home and seeing Lucille reminded her of a question she forgot to ask her the last time they met.

"Next in line," Gwen said as Lucille smiled and pushed her items down the slowmoving conveyer belt.

"Gwen, how ya' doin'?"

"Let me tell you, girl! They trying to work me like a Hebrew slave!" Then Gwen looked behind her to see a gentleman putting his full basket on the belt. "Excuse me, sir... this line is closed.

She'll help you over there."

"Gwen, I don't see how you do it. I couldn't be no cashier. This ain't for me!"

Gwen shook her head, "I need the money. That's the only reason why. I'd rather be home sleeping. Oh, by the way, before I forget! Do you know anyone who has a room for rent? It could be an apartment."

Lucille was silent for a moment, "No, I can't think of anyone. The only thing I can think of is my church's side house, but ain't no one been in there for long, long time. The deacons' boarded up the windows. But, the pastor told my mother that he wanted to rent it out if he couldn't sell it." "Does it have four walls and a roof?" "I suppose so. Do you want my mother to ask the pastor about it?" "Would you?'

*** *** ***

This morning, Gwen politely declined George's invitation to drive her to work. She told him that Xavier was coming by.

A few minutes later, Xavier pulled up and Gwen met him outside. Their kiss, after she got in his car, was met with a with a disapproving smirk on Orangie's face, who was now standing next to George at the front door.

"Did you tell grandmother that you found a place?" "No."

"No! Why? She's gonna find out sooner or later. Wouldn't that make her feel better about you?" "She's never gonna like me no matter what I do. I don't wanna tell her anything until I pay the pastor all of the rent money to move in, in case something happens and he changes his mind. Besides, I want to do this myself. I don't want them knowing where I'm going. All they know is that I'm going to work this morning."

"What about next week? You pay the man the last installment this morning, what are you going do next week when I'm outta town?" "I'm gonna do what I gotta do."

*** *** ***

The parsonage (as the affluent white congregations would call it) was located in the little sublet town of Guthrie. Guthrie was, technically, a part of Princeton but the sparely populated town was located a couple of miles off the expressway, hidden mostly by small, rolling hills. Most of the residents there knew few people outside of their area, only crossing paths in Kroger's.

The pastor, whose name Gwen quickly forgot, was well into his eighties. It took him a few minutes to return with key and a few moments of fumbling before the key fit in the hole. He leaned in and used his body weight to push the door open. The loud creaking sound revealed to Gwen that she would have a lot of work to do.

"It ain't much, my dear," the pastor said as he struggled to get the key out of the door, "but I hope you like it. We haven't used this place for... goodness sake, nearing twenty years, I guess."

The door opened even wider behind the pastor who was facing Gwen but it was difficult to see what laid beyond it.

"Now, as I said the other day, it's gonna need some work but I think it would be a nice place for anyone who wants some peace and quiet."

Gwen tried peering into the dark, but wasn't able to see but a foot in front of the doorway. She looked at Xavier, who looked to her and shrugged his shoulders. She looked to Lucille, who only looked down to her feet.

"Pastor, can I see what's inside?"

"Oh, yes dear. I'm sorry. I'm here going on and on. Let me see where this light switch is." He leaned back and moved his hand up and down the wall on the left-side. "Ahh, here it is!" The click of the switch echoed in the dark room, then suddenly a flickering light appeared in the middle of the room. The pastor walked in and waved from them to follow.

She stepped in the doorway and stuck her head in and slowly looked around. She stepped back and looked at Xavier. She put both hands over her mouth.

Aunt Minerva stood looking out of the livingroom window. She only slightly separated the drapes as to not let the couple who were parked in the car in front of the house know of her presence.

West came out of the car first, then Sandy followed after checking the locked doors on her car. West stuck his neck in through the door before turning to Sandy.

"It's cool. Come in, ain't nobody here!"

"Your aunt has a beautiful home," she said in a soft tone.

"Why, thank you! I worked many, many years to get this!" Aunt Minerva said that while standing a few feet away in the shadow of the hallway.

"Aunt Minerva! What are you doing here? I mean, I didn't expect you home so soon!"

"I see that. Well, aren't you going to introduce me to your friend?"

"Oh, ahhh... this is Sandy. She's a friend from school and... and she... we.. .we're... we're here to study for a test." West looked at Sandy with a blank look on his face.

Before Sandy could think of a complimentary answer, she saw

Aunt Minerva wiping her hands on her apron. "Don't bother young lady, I already know what you two are up to. Besides, I know when West Jr. talks about studying, he's up to something."

Aunt Minerva walked past them and into the kitchen. "Sandy, right? I know you and West Jr. are an item. He doesn't think I hear him talking to you when I'm in the other room."

West's mouth was opened.

"Now, are you two just going to stand there or are you going to sit down here so I can give you something to eat?"

"Thank you, ma'am!"

"Yes, but Aunt Minerva, I thought we would-"

"Go to your room," Minerva said turning around with a boiling kettle in her hand.

"No! West, Jr you are not taking this young lady to your room in my house. It's either the kitchen or the livingroom, but not any further. You're not grown in my house!"

"Yes, Auntie."

*** *** ***

Aunt Minerva made West and Sandy some hot chocolate and prepared a small plate of buttered toast, scrambled eggs and bacon.

"Miss Minerva, that was delicious. Thank you so much!"

"Dear, you can call me Aunt Minerva." Looking at West, "All of his friends do, even the ones I don't like. Alright now, before I let you study in the living room. I want to talk to you about being your own person."

West took a deep breath, then rolled his eyes.

"Now, West, Jr., I'm really talking about you. So, you don't go gettin' impatient with me. I know you like this young lady and," looking at Sandy, "the key to anything you value in life to give it 100 percent. Not 50 percent, not 80 percent. Give your all! Don't let people talk down or try to talk you out of it. You see this house here? Ever since I was a little girl, I knew I wanted to own my own home. I would sit down by a tree out in the field at lunchtime and imagined myself in my own place. Not sharing a bedroom with all of my sisters. As I got older, every job I got, I saved a few dollars here and a few dollars there. When I saw an opportunity to invest in a business or loaned money, I always saw a profit."

"Aunt Minerva, we wanna study," West said while holding up his face by leaning on the table.

"Boy, you better stop leaning on my table! You know how much that cost me?"

West slowly leaned back in his chair.

"Be honest with yourself and be honest with people. People will trust you because they'll feel that you're a good bet!

"Okay, that's all I've got to say for now. When you two are finished, West Jr. I want you to wash those dishes, I've gotta get those clothes off the line."

Aunt Minerva loosened her apron, draping it over one of the chairs and walked down the hallway to the backdoor.

Sandy looked at West, "I left my books in the car, should I get them?"

"Naw, let's sit here for a few minutes, Aunt Minerva usually remembers that she needs something from the store and she'll go running out the door!"

Not more than five minutes passed when the sound of Minerva's shoes paraded by them. "Now, West Junior, I forgot I need to get some more detergent and some Ajax. I'll be back in a few minutes."

"Yes, Auntie," West said smiling while tugging Sandy to follow him as the taxi that picked up Aunt Minerva drove off."

Gwen felt a sharp pain in her neck. She rolled over to her other side and felt the hard, wooden floor just beneath it. It took a moment before she opened her eyes for her to realize she fell asleep in the same spot she sat after scrubbing the walls.

She leaned up, looking toward the sound of voices that was coming from somewhere around her. Her eyes were still blurry but she made out one of the figures to be Xavier, who was sitting on a small stool that was near the old, rusted stove. He was strumming a few chords on his wooden guitar to Lucille, whom was standing adjacent to him.

"What time is it?"

"Oh, you're up! It's about 10," Xavier said as he leaned the guitar to the stove. He reached down to give Gwen a hand up.

"Wait! Wait a minute. My neck hurts!"

"Gwen, I told you, you should sleep at Grandmother's house until this is done. You can't get everything done in a day."

"You don't understand. Mrs. Strain don't want me there. You know that. Besides, the sooner I finish, the sooner I can get some furniture and a bed in here. I have to buy all this stuff. I don't have anyone giving me everything I ask for."

"Now Gwen, don't say that. They like you. You just don't know them that well. They're real good people. Grandmother just needs more time."

Gwen made her way to her feet. "I don't need anybody's pity and I certainly don't need her handout. I can do it on my own."

"Hi, Gwen," Lucille said in meek voice. "I just came by to see if you needed anything. I knocked on the door but when you didn't answer so I came in."

"Can you clean? Can you paint?"

"Oh Gwen, I'm so sorry, I can't right now. Momma was sending out to run some errands but I decided to see you first. I'm supposed to be there already. I can help you later on, if you need me?"

"Yeah, Gwen, me too! Me and Grandfather gotta go into town to pick up a few things for Grandmother. I borrowed his car while mine is being repaired, just so I can check up on you. I gotta go, but I'll be back later. Okay?"

"Oh, so it's like that then! Don't worry, I got this. I don't need none of y'all. I can do it myself."

Lucille waved to Gwen as she walked briskly out. Gwen, momentarily distracted, received a quick kiss on the lips by Xavier as he too sprinted out of the house. "I'm gonna give her a ride down the hill. I'll see you later!"

"Xavier… Xavier," Gwen screamed as she too raced to the doorway. "I've got something very important to tell you!"

"Gwen, I promise… I promise, I'll be back soon. Se you later,"

Xavier said as the car started to drive off.

A million things went through her mind, the same million that she was struggling to hold back from coming out of her mouth. She walked toward the small pail of dirty water. She reached in, grabbing a sponge that was more oily and gritty than the floor she slipped on the first night she walked in.

She wiped her forehead with her forearm, thinking about why she was there. It was about a week to the day, she gave the pastor the first month's rent. She remembered the exhilaration of receiving the key. It was the first time in many years where the keys to a room meant freedom. She looked past the morbid, murky brownish grey walls and the musty, smell that made its way up her nostrils and through her lungs and in her brain.

This was her freedom, but it was going to cost her.

There was a knock at the door.

"Who is it? Xavier, don't come around here playing games." She got up and peeked out of the window. Outside stood Ollie, Lucille's youngest brother.

"Good morning, Miss Gwen. I… I just stopped by to see if I can give you a hand. I can do anything you need, just ask and I'll do it."

"Isn't that sweet! Ollie! Please, please come in." She looked around the room then back to him. She crossed her arms.

"Yes, ma'am."

"Do you have any weed?"

Two weeks had passed but it felt like just one day since Gwen started to renovate the old parsonage. She didn't have the conversation with him she wanted. He was either too busy or discussions about getting out of Orangie's home dominated their time. She worried still about the growing enormity of it and moving into the parsonage didn't lessen it.

She heard a knock on the door and instinctively she thought it was Ollie. He came over every morning before she went to work. He wanted to know if there was anything he could help her with since she was almost always by herself. For her, he was a pleasant distraction. She often wondered if they were the same age, what would her life be like.

Before she could make it to the door, someone was knocking again. To her surprise, it was Lucille. She was carrying a large covered tray. The aluminum foil concealed something that was giving off a lot of steam.

"Hi Gwen, I thought I'd stop by and bring you and Xavier some cookies."

"Come in. Xavier's not here." Taking the tray from Lucille, "He's never around when you need him."

"Oh, I thought he was sleeping over."

"He did but he left in the middle of the night to jam with his band. He has to play with his friends but I can't get him to fix the cabinets over there."

"Can't get who to fix what," a voice said behind them.

Gwen and Lucille turned around and saw Xavier smiling as he stood in the doorway, while holding a bottle of orange juice."

"Well, if it ain't Mister Rolling Stone. How long are you here for?"

"Aww Gwen, why you wanna do me like that? You know I gotta spend time with my boys. I hardly see them cause I'm always with you or with Grandmother or plain work!"

"Hi, Xavier," Lucille interrupted. Gwen looked at her and saw the expression on her face then saw Xavier's reaction. "Hey Lucille, how you doin'?" "Fine. I brought some chocolate chip cookies."

"You remembered! Hey, that's great!"

Gwen walked up to a chair that was next to Xavier and leaned her weight on to it. "I've been wanting to talk to you for so long and you keep giving me excuses. When can we sit down and talk about a few things?"

"I know, I know, I know! You wanna know when am I gonna finally move outta Grandmother's house!"

Gwen looked around the room then turned to him, "Are you coming by here tonight?"

He stared at her for a second, "Yeah, I'm coming here tonight. He kissed her on the forehead and started to walk off until he saw the tray on the counter. He grabbed a handful of cookies and walked briskly out of the door.

Gwen looked down to her feet then took a deep breath. "Did you sleep with my man?"

"What!"

Gwen turned all the way around to face her. "I said, did you sleep with Xavier?"

Lucille looked away.

"Are you going to answer me?"

"Yes."

"Yes, what?"

"We did it." Lucille looked into Gwen's eyes. "I'm sorry, Gwen. I didn't mean to hurt you. I'm so sorry. Please forgive me. I want us to be friends."

"You want to be my friend after you slept with my man?"

There was silence in the room. Both women refused to move: Gwen, because she didn't trust herself and Lucille, because she didn't want to risk giving Gwen any ideas.

"Let me ask you just one more question. Where did this happen? Don't tell me this happened here in my house?"

"No. Xavier said we should meet at this place downtown."

"Oh, I see. Okay, I'll handle it from here. I don't hate you, but I'll never trust you and I don't want you coming back here."

Lucille slowly walked out of the house, crying.

Gwen followed and stopped at the doorway and yelled at her, "Don't say anything to nobody about this especially Xavier."

*** *** ***

The day had gone by and Gwen returned home after her shift from the Dollar store was done.

She paced up and down the length of the cottage, wondering the best way to confront him. She often looked at the clock imagining where he was at any given time. She played several different scenarios in her mind, none of them ended well for Xavier.

The door opened and Xavier walked in carrying a small bag of groceries. He reached into the bag and put a few items in the fridge before walking over to Gwen and giving her a kiss.

"Okay, I know why you're mad but I'm late because I had to stop by the check-cashing place."

"I'm not mad about that. But, I am mad."

"Why? Oh, I know… because I'm a spoiled brat and I refuse to grow up."

"That's true… but I'm angry that you lied to me. You took me for granted and you took advantage of me cause you knew that because of my situation, I was vulnerable."

"What more do you want me to say? Look, I'm sorry. Alright? I'm sorry."

"You're sorry and I'm pregnant."

"Pregnant? How? When?"

Gwen's face was expressionless. "To make matters worse, you spend as little time over here as possible. As you know, I have a lot of things to do to get this place where I'm comfortable. Yet, you don't have time to help me but you have time to have sex with Lucille."

"Wait… who said I was having sex with Lucille? Gwen, stop imagining things. It must be this pregnancy thing, it's got you thinking crazy."

"I'm not crazy. Pregnant, yes. Crazy, no. Don't try to pretend that I don't know what I'm talking about. I saw how you too looked at each other."

"Gwen-"

"Ah, Ah, Ah. No! Don't even start! I confronted her this morning after you left. She confessed and she told me everything including the part where you told her to meet you at the motel downtown. And, for her to wait for you on the bench next to the park."

Xavier bowed his head.

"Okay," Gwen said. "I'm gonna make this easy on you. Here's your ring back. I don't want this baby any more than you do. I don't wanna be trapped being connected to you or your grandmother Orangie. I'm so over the both of you.

"So, this is what we're gonna do. You're gonna pay for me to go to Charleston. You're gonna pay for a room for me for three days and you're gonna pay for the abortion. And, you're gonna pay for my time off from work."

"Gwen, it don't have to end this way. I can be a good dad."

"How can you be a good dad when you're still a kid?"

"I expect you back here in two days with all of the money. I don't care how you get it but you better be back here in two days or else. Now get all of your things and get out. This is Gwen's place."

Gwen looked around the room. She was happy. Most of the walls had been scrubbed free of the ash buildup. The air was noticeably fresher, even the interior seemed to have gotten larger. But, still she had work to do. The house needed painting. Then, she felt, she could finally say, *"It's my place!"*

The thought hadn't fully settled in her mind when she realized that she still had most of her things over at Orangie's. She'd have to face her after breaking up with Xavier a few weeks ago. *"I wonder if Xavier told her about the baby?"* She reasoned it away by telling herself that it didn't matter because she's her own person and not Orangie's ward.

She lifted up her blouse and looked at her stomach. She still felt the grips they attached to her that afternoon. *"Was it the right decision?"* She sat down on the couch and cried. She blew her nose. "I'm NOT living with Orangie anymore! I'm NOT going to be spoken down to anymore! I'm NOT going to be trapped in a relationship with a lazy man who only has time to smoke weed and chase as many skirts as he can find in a day!" She blew her nose once again. No, it wasn't the right decision, she thought to herself, but it was the only choice.

The afternoon came and went.

So, did the evening.

And, a few weeks.

And…

A few months.

Gwen lay on her new bed, looking up at the ceiling. The house was quiet. The air was still except for the sound of the branches swaying from the early evening breeze.

She found respite but she also found loneliness.

She thought about her daughter and her mother in Madisonville, remembering all of the mischief she caused. She found herself laughing hysterically about the time she lied about eating all of her grandmother's chocolate chip cookies.

She turned over and reached for her box of mementos. She flipped through the first set of pictures that lay on top of the pile while going through the full gamut of emotions. She put the pictures aside, and then dug into the box looking for another set until she came upon the last letter she received from her great-grandaunt when she was still at Pence.

She took a deep breath because she knew she hadn't finished it. She remembered hearing her aunt's voice as she read each word and knew that she was saying more to her than about the issue of her younger sister getting pregnant or about Michael getting his M.A. before he was twenty-five or even about her mother's boyfriend murdering a co-worker in their livingroom in front of a newborn. It was much, much more than that.

She pulled the small bundle of paper from the envelope and proceeded to eyeball each page from top to bottom looking for that ending point.

She found it. It was there, right next to a state trooper's footprint.

A few words into the new paragraph and Gwen knew the horrors were about to begin again.

24

She flipped through the pages of the letter her grand-aunt sent, from top to bottom, looking for something to indicate where she left off. She didn't want to re-read from the beginning and relive the pain of those moments again.

She took a sigh of relief, then sat up against the head of the bed. The passage started like this:

"Phyllis met a man, you may have met him, his name was General Lee. I don't know if that was his real name or not. He was an older man, I'd say in his 60's. Phyllis had just turned 20.

"He used to say all these nice things to her: promising to take care of her and her son. She got to liking him. Then your mother's boyfriend was getting out of jail. That's the same guy who shot his friend and took his money and the car keys— that one! Your mother invited him to live at her house with her and your brothers and sisters.

"Phyllis was terrified because she hadn't forgotten how that creep pointed a gun at her and her baby just after he shot the man dead.

"Well, to make a long story short, she and her son moved in with General Lee. He took them in and I have to admit, he did a lot for them. He really was a nice man.

"Now, one weekend, I think it was on a Sunday. General Lee had a party and had the neighbors over. Everything was fine up until

Phyllis' baby father showed up.

"Phyllis didn't know he was there. She was in the kitchen cleaning up. She heard General Lee come through the house and walked to their bedroom. She didn't know the baby's father was asking to see his son.

"Phyllis walked into the bedroom and saw General Lee loading his gun. She asked him what was he doing and he refused to answer her but kept on loading his gun. She ran over to him and started to argue with him to put the gun away. They struggled and the gun went off.

"General Lee fell on the floor between the bed and the dresser. "She called the police but when they arrived, General Lee was dead.

"The police questioned her about what happened and she panicked. She ran outside and drove off in the police car.

"She drove a few miles away before they caught her.

"They ended up charging her with manslaughter."

Gwen stopped reading at this point and looked at the number of pages left to be read. She realized there was a lot more family drama that she was about to hear.

But, she thought to herself, not tonight.

She wrestled with insomnia. It had everything to do with reading about Phyllis that kept her up all night. With every word and every affliction Phyllis went through, Gwen felt the impulse of those confrontations and wounds of those blows.

In between those thoughts, she remembered that she was no longer with Xavier and all she had to look forward to was her dead-end job at the dollar-store.

The distant sound of car horns jolted her attention. She looked down to her feet, not caring that she'd stain her bleached, white socks on the wood floor. However, the allure of fresh, hot tea made all the sense in the world at that moment.

A thousand thoughts seeped between the steam from her cup. She looked for the answers between the opaque images that swirled around her spoon. She wished for a different life. She wished she could do her life all over again. She wondered for a moment, then she thought if she could do it all over, she wouldn't come back as a little black girl growing up dirt-poor in a small town in Kentucky with a big family in the middle of nowhere.

What if she were born white? What if she were an only child? What would it be like if she were a little white girl with long blond hair with a handsome father and a pretty mother? What if she had her own room with toys everywhere and a closet full of clothes? What would it be like if she could look out her bedroom window and she her backyard stretch for miles and miles. What would she be now?

She noticed a folded newpaper on the chair adjacent to hers. She didn't remember how it got there but a name on the header triggered her attention. *"Connie!" Connie... Connie, why is that name so familiar, she thought.*

Then it came to her.

She ran to the bedroom and came back with her bag. She withdrew a small, tattered little book. Many of the leaves were torn from the spine and a number of lines had strikethrough, some the contacts were illegible but after turning and shoving back loosed papers, she came across the name that she had been looking for.

She took a sip of tea, then cradled the phone receiver on her neck as she examined a number written in the book. "Hello? Is this Constance? Hi! I know you don't remember me but my name is Gwen, we met back in Charleston a few years ago...."

"Gwen! Gwen!" A voice called out from a silver Continental that just pulled up to the Greyhound bus.

Gwen smiled and waved at Constance, while pulling her bags from the open compartment of the bus.

The drive from the stop to Connie's Place was not more than ten minutes in light traffic. They talked about old times but Gwen was surprised that Constance had not spoken with her cousin Delores (or as Gwen called her, Miss D) in quite a few years. It struck her strange because both women were alike in a lot of ways.

The car pulled up to a red-bricked building with a large neon sign that read, CONNIE'S PLACE. There were no windows on the building save the door that lead into the restaurant-bar.

Once inside, Gwen saw the dance-floor on the right. It stretched from just right of the door way all the way to the back of the building. The middle section had tables and chairs and on the left was a circle bar with stools in front of it. For a late morning, the place was almost full.

As the women made their way through the tables, Gwen, following Connie, saw two heavyset women who were seated at a table nearest to the bar. They raised their rum glasses to Connie. As Gwen passed by them, she noticed both of the women had large shopping bags on the empty seats adjacent to them.

Connie looked at Gwen, "You can put your things down in that room. Go through the door and my office is on the right. I need to take care of some business here before we go home. Make yourself at home and I'll be with you in a few minutes."

"Okay!" Gwen put her bags down in front of her, "Oh, Connie… where is the ladies' room?"

Connie pointed to the right side in the corner of the dance area, just to the side of the jukebox.

Gwen didn't worry about her bags left unattended as she felt it was safe in her friend's establishment. She returned from the bathroom and walked to the back room with her bags. As she went through the door, she passed the two heavyset women who were now standing in the doorway of Connie's office. They were pulling out new clothing like a Christian Dior blouse and a Gucci diamond-studded belt. The department store tags twirling under the office lights.

She softly took a few steps passed them and heard Connie's voice, "Okay, I'll take this one. That olive green blouse would look great on me. It compliments my complexion… and, I'll take these two pants. How much for all of these?"

She carefully placed her bags on the ground at the end of the hallway and crept passed the door, unbeknownst to the women in the meeting. She sat at the bar and asked for a glass of coke.

A few moments later, the three women came out and found Gwen finishing a burger platter.

"Gwen, I'm so sorry! I totally forgot all about you. Are you all right?"

"I'm okay. I'm just tired from the bus ride."

Connie smiled then turned to the two women. "It was nice to seeing you again! Let's do lunch again real soon?"

One of the women chuckled, "Yes, Miss Connie, we'll do lunch again real soon!"

*** *** ***

Some hours had passed but Gwen said nothing about the incident. She wanted to see if Connie would let her in by herself. In between the brief exchanges that Connie had with her bar customers, Gwen talked about her plans, Xavier, the Strains' and Pence.

Connie looked at the clock and shouted, "WE'RE CLOSING UP IN AN HOUR! IF YOU WANT SOMETHING TO EAT, ORDER NOW BECAUSE WE START BREAKING DOWN IN HALF AN HOUR!"

Just as she finished her announcement, a tall man, about 6 feet came into the restaurant. He was a handsome man of about 30, clean-shaven, pressed dress shirt, navy slacks and brown wingtip shoes.

Connie shook her head and draped a towel over her shoulder after she finished washing the last dirty glass. "No, Bosie! Don't think you're gonna come in here and hold us up from an hour with your nonsense. We're closing the door in an hour."

"C'mon, Miss Connie," Bosie said, "You know, I only want one drink. You can't do me like this! I'm one of your favorite customers!"

"Favorite customer, alright?" Connie stared at him for a second.

Bosie stared back at her for a second before he started smiling.

"Okay, one drink! But, that's it, Bosie. Only one!"

"Hey, Miss Connie… who's this cute one here?"

"You don't worry, yourself. She ain't no one you gonna know. Now, here's your one and only drink. Go over to the jukebox and play something for me while I clean up this counter."

Bosie walked away but smiled at Gwen as he headed toward the other end of the restaurant.

"Gwen, don't worry about him. He ain't your type. Bosie's crazy!"

Gwen heard the words behind her, but smiled at the character whose bad-boy smirk intrigued her.

Slivers of sunlight came through the slats in Gwen's room. The glare awakened her. She stretched all of her limbs to the limit. She thought to herself, Sundays ought to be a mandatory stay-in-bed holiday.

The scent of roasting coffee invited her to get up. She slid her feet into her pink bunny slippers, twisted the cold, bedroom doorknob and took thirteen steps downstairs to a woman pouring a pitcher of boiling, black liquid into a large white mug.

'Connie, are you okay?"

"Uh, huh! I'm just trying to get some of this caffeine in me before I run out of here." She turned Gwen, "Why don't you move here? I was just thinking. I could use the help. Besides, you could start a new life here and you'll have friends who'll look after you."

It suddenly dawned on Gwen that maybe Connie was right. She had a dead-end job, a brokedown loser of an ex-boyfriend and she wouldn't have to see Orangie's and George's rank faces. She'd only lose her place and the few items she had inside. She weighed the costs, then exhaled.

"Well, what do you think? A fresh start? Friends and a job with me as long as you want? "

"Do you really need my help? I mean, I never worked in a restaurant before. What would I do?"

"You could bartend. It's easy. I can teach you. Having you behind the counter will give me more time to do office work."

"Okay! Okay… I'm in. When do I start?"

"NOW. Go upstairs and shower. I'm leaving out of here in fifteen minutes."

Gwen's first few days were a mixture of fear and excitement, jealous stares and flirtatious comments. A guy sitting at the bar or a group sitting at a table whistling at her was met the typical response, *"Oh no! You see, if it's you, then I know you don't have what it takes, but if I'm interested, then I'll let you know 'cause I'll know it's real and it's on."*

*** *** ***

CONNIE'S PLACE was a different type of bar. It wasn't like Candyman's or The Last Chance. This felt more like a place for grown folks, not for the area's "in crowd."

The late afternoon rush normally began at four. Many people came by just before or just after work to have a drink or have a burger platter before going home. Some came for some "down home cooking" or because they didn't want to face what was waiting at home. Either way, Connie was the homegirl that everyone enjoyed seeing upon entering.

Gwen, herself, began to notice the regulars and pointed to them and calling out their drinks. She came to know their faces, their dress. She smiled when she realized that she was building a mental dossier of Connie's customers the way the bartenders at The Last Dance and Candyman's had of her.

One afternoon, Gwen was drying a glass behind the counter when she looked at her watch. She patiently watched the second hand on her watch made it up the 60 second mark. She looked at the entrance, when the door opened on cue. There he stood. Same time. Every day. No words had passed between them. She knew him through the playful bantering he'd have with Connie when he walked in. But, something different happened this day. Something, Gwen hadn't expected. Bosie made a beeline for her, ignoring Connie's daily salutation.

"I know, I haven't formally introduced myself to you. My name's Nate but my friends call me, Bosie! I know your name. You're Gwen, right?"

"You have good ears. So, Mister Bosie, what can I get you?"

"How about some good conversation? I don't get that around here other than Connie telling me, That's enough, Bosie! Bosie, it's time to leave!"

"Maybe she's right. She's probably letting everybody know, you're trouble!"

"Awww! Don't say that. I'm a nice guy. As you could see… I work, I have one drink with a meal. I don't cause any problems. If I did, don't you think Connie wouldn't let me back in here?"

"You've got a point." Gwen leaned her head back, eyeing him down from head to toe. "You might be nicely dressed and have a cute smile, but that doesn't mean you're not a bad boy."

"I never thought about that. Maybe you're right. That just means that I need to work a little harder to persuade you that I'm worth getting to know."

"Oh, really! You look at me and think I'm that gullible and will fall for any guy's rap?"

"No stories, just the truth. The truth about who I am, what I'm about and where I'm going. And maybe, just maybe, there might be a position for a woman like yourself by me."

"You're slick! You think you have what it takes to have a woman like me? I'm not like the women you're met before. My world's a whole lot bigger. It takes a lot to deal with my situation!"

"Okay, Miss Gwen. In case you didn't know, I've been to 'Nam. I've got an engineering degree and I take care of my mother. I think I can deal with anything you going on."

Gwen crossed her arms.

Bosie smiled, "Tell you what. Since I'm always coming in here to eat, why don't you let me take you out to get something to eat?"

"When?"

"How about now?"

Gwen turned around to see Connie slowly shaking her head before turning around to help another customer.

"Okay. But, we have to be back before we close. You think you can handle that?"

"I think I can handle anything."

28

"Thanks for dinner. How did you know I love this place?" Gwen held Bosie's face.

"Because you always tell me this is your favorite place, everytime we come here!"

"Oh, I see you were listening!"

"I listen. You just don't think I am, but I am. Okay, changing the subject. So, where are you at?"

"What do you mean," Gwen said as she leaned against the passenger-side door.

"I mean, we've been dating for three months now, I feel that it's time that you come and meet my family. Now, before you say anything, I know that you wanted some time to prepare yourself, but I really want you to meet everybody especially, mother."

"I know. I haven't forgotten. I've been thinking about that very thing while I was getting ready tonight. And, I feel okay about it. We can go and see them anytime you'd like."

"Well, how about now? It'll only be for a few minutes and it would put mother at ease about the woman I've been spending so much of my time with."

Gwen paused for a second as she looked into his eyes. Hmmm, she thought, that's strange, I never heard anybody call their mother, mother. Gwen was more intrigued than uncomfortable with having to face an unknown environment. She paused before because she wondered what about her life and her past had Bosie shared with them? How would she defend it?

"I'm ready. I'll be glad to meet your mother and the rest of your family." They were just a few blocks away from Connie's house but Bosie sped up and made a sharp U-turn and headed toward his home.

"Gwen, I've been looking forward to this for a very long time. You don't know how happy I am for you to finally meet everybody. I told them all about you!"

"All about me?"

"Yeah, I told them that you used to live in Charleston and you went to school there and you're a hard-worker and everything!"

The car pulled up to the house yet Gwen felt unsettled. She decided that she'd keep as much of her life as they'd say, close-to-the-chest, in case anything started to kick up.

She held Bosie's hand as they walked up the path toward the door. Bosie was rambling on about something she didn't hear. The only voice she heard was her own, and it was telling her: Be as evasive as possible. You've got a life and a reputation to protect!

It was no more than a few minutes after Bosie's family warmly invited her in that Gwen felt safe enough to exhale. She liked the fact that Bosie hugged and kissed his sisters and helped his mother to sit down on the couch and helped her to get up so that she might check on how dinner was coming along. Everytime she turned around to see Bosie's mother, she was greeted with a warm smile.

Bosie, who was sitting just to her right, got up to take a phone call in another room. It seemed to be about his son and the reason why he wasn't dropped off by the baby momma. It was then that Bosie's mother, motioned for Gwen to help her get up to go to the kitchen.

"Gwen, I'm so happy you came by tonight. We heard so much about you. You, indeed, are such a beautiful woman. Please come with me to the kitchen, I've got something to ask you."

"Oh, sure. I'm so happy you like me. I was worried that you wouldn't."

The two women walked past the doorway where Bosie was talking loudly on the phone.

"My dear, The Lord has a plan for each of us, and He has a plan for you and me."

Gwen handed her a burgundy pot handle holder, "I believe that, too."

"Do you really, my dear?"

"Yes, I do."

"Well, whoever gets my son will need a lot of prayer."

Gwen was ready to reply when the weight of that comment hit her. She smiled then helped her back to the living room. No words passed between them until it was time for Bosie to take her home.

*** *** ***

Gwen didn't give Bosie a reason why she didn't want to go out for a couple of weeks afterwards, despite seeing him afterwork at Connie's during the week. Over time Bosie would inquire; Gwen's answer was always the same: "Everything's fine. I just need some space!"

He'd walk away sullen, knowing something had to have happened that night at his home but no one at home knew what he was asking about. He was perplexed and his facial expressions spoke volumes.

One day, the regular stream of customers came but she noticed that Bosie hadn't come in at his usual time. That was strange, she thought. Bosie was one of the most punctual people she had ever met. It was one of those things that she could count on and it spoke to her about his commitment.

Another hour had passed and she wondered if she forgot about an appointment that he may have mentioned, but she forgot. She threw off any suggestions that he was going elsewhere for a drink. Connie got her attention while holding the phone receiver on her neck. She pointed across the room to several empty glasses that needed to be picked up.

Gwen put down the towel she had been drying the glasses with and walked from behind the bar just as Bosie walked in. His shirt was open, exposing some chest hairs. His hair was unraveled and his eyes were bloodshot red. The smell of rum preceded the scent of his Halston cologne.

Bosie stumbled and pushed people out of his way as he walked toward the bar. He didn't seem to notice that he pushed Gwen out of the way, as well. "CONNIE… CONNIE… I'M TALKING TO YOU! GIVE ME A DOUBLE."

Connie put her hand over the receiver, "Bosie, go home! You've had enough!"

"I WANT A DRINK!"

"BO- SIE! I said, GO HOME!"

A few feet away, Gwen had watched the interaction while collecting the dirty glasses. She carefully made her way through the crowd but didn't want to incite Bosie by confronting him. She felt better that Connie was taking the lead.

Bosie stared at Connie for a second, he raised his hand and flipped his middle finger at her, "BITCH!" He turned around and walked through the crowd. To the side, he saw a man and woman seated on stools having a drink and bobbing their heads to the Parliament-Funkadelic song that was playing on the jukebox.

He stared at them for a few seconds until he walked behind the woman. He reached down and pinched her rear-end.

Connie and Gwen looked on in horror.

Connie dropped the phone and rushed for the swinging door at the side of the bar. Connie held on to her chest for a second before pointing to the exit. "BOSIE… BOSIE… GET OUT! GET OUT!"

Some moved out the way so Bosie could get out CONNIE'S.

Bosie looked around, looking at all of the faces staring back at him. He saw Gwen in the back, standing by herself, crying. He turned and looked at the crowd, with Connie in the middle with her arms crossed.

"I think a few days away from here will be a good thing for us."

Bosie looked at Gwen, "A good thing? I'm fine, it ain't me. People just don't know how to act and I gotta correct 'em."

"Oh," Gwen said as she adjusted herself on the seat next to the window of their Greyhound bus, "so… you think grabbing that married woman's butt in front of her husband was her acting up?"

"No, what I'm saying is—," Bosie shook his head, "nevermind! I see I can't win with you."

"I'm on your side, babe. That's why we're going to Charleston. They've got everything there. You can be the man you wanna be. You'll see!" Gwen softly prodded his rib with her elbow. "It won't be no time before everybody knows you're *The Man!*"

Bosie said nothing but stretched his hands above him then locked his hands behind his head. "Wake me up when we're in paradise, okay?"

"Smarty-pants," she grumbled.

*** *** ***

Charleston looked similar but something seemed off. It was almost five years since she left her old stompin' ground, but it seemed like just a shell of its old existence.

Gone were the familiar buildings on Court Street. No more Candyman's, no more The Last Chance nightclubs.

As they walked hand-in-hand down the street, she kept looking out for some familiar faces but she didn't recognize any. As they approached a motel with a sign affixed just over the door. It read, Great Daily and Weekly Rates. Gwen thought to herself, maybe it's all for the better. I could have a fresh start here too!"

The hallway leading up to their room was musty and the scent of the hallway overheating air conditioner made things all the worse.

Bosie carried all of the bags into the room and laid them on the bed. Gwen held on to the bureau that was just inside of the doorway.

"Give me a minute to catch myself. All of a sudden, I feel so dizzy."

Bosie turned and put all of the bags on the floor, then turned back the covers for Gwen to lay down. He carried her to the bed and removed her shoes.

"You want something to drink? I can see if they have something downstairs?"

"No…no, I just need to rest. Do me a favor, give me my bag. I need you to run down to Rite-Aid and pick me up some aspirin and some flu medicine. Here's $5, bring me back my change."

"Okay, I'll be back soon."

"You know where it is right? Two street blocks back and across the street. You'll see the sign as you get close to it. Hurry back and don't get lost."

Gwen drifted off to sleep. Occasionally, she'd turn over. The perspiration felt like a blanket over her. Each time, she'd notice the daylight getting a bit dimmer each time she'd look up. But, each time she'd notice that Bosie hadn't returned.

A couple of hours later, she turned over but this time the night sky was just out her window and her room was completely dark.

Gwen reached over to the nightstand and grabbed her watch. The glare from the street light reflected off the face and dials. It was almost 9:20 p.m.

She looked back around, "Bosie!" There was no response. "Bosie! Bosie?" She leaned over to the right side. That side of the bed was in pristine condition.

She sat up in bed and peered around the room. As far as she was able to make out, she was alone. She slumped back in the pillows. She noticed the cold, damp spots. Despite her throbbing headache, she turned the pillow over and fell back asleep.

Gwen slowly opened her eyes. Seeing the bright daylight outside her window, she struggled but was able to sit up in bed. She looked at her watch again. She shook her head as she looked at the bags that were still on the floor at the foot of the bed. She walked over to the sink and washed her face. Slowly, she grabbed her bag and pulled out some bills from inside. She shoved the bills in her pocket, slid her feet into her slippers and walked out the door. She struggled with the thought of going to the nearest drugstore or finding the nearest wateringhole where Bosie was most likely at.

She walked without direction until she found herself over at SPYRO'S bar on Summer's Street. It was the last remnant of the bars from Gwen's younger days.

Two days had passed since Gwen and Bosie arrived in Charleston. It was also two days, roughly, since she last saw him.

Before she left the hotel room, she spread out all of the money she had on the bed and did a rough mental calculation of how far this money would last. She needed to find Bosie or find work immediately so that they might move there permanently after the holidays.

She walked inside and saw an all-male band. An African-American band to boot! They were playing some funk music. She felt more at-ease. She looked around and saw some vaguely familiar faces. They looked like people she knew but she couldn't place a name with those faces. They definitely didn't fit into the Friends category.

"Gwen," a voice called. "Gwen, is that you?"

Gwen walked over to the booth with several women. "Yeah, it's me!"

"I thought it was you. I was just telling her that I thought I saw you walking down the street the other day with a new guy. Then I saw him later that night, right over there talking with Nancy and Marcine Phillips!"

"Nancy… Marcine… they're still around!"

"Girl, you don't know the half of it. They're still selling. Nancy was over in that corner kissing and touching all over him!"

Gwen stood frozen.

"About a hot minute later, they went to the women's bathroom and after they came out, they left."

"Oh, really! Any of you got her number?"

"Yeah, I think I got it. I'm a businesswoman, you understand."

Gwen took the gum wrapper that the number was on and walked over to the phone booth that was on the other side of the bar. It was still pretty loud, but she didn't want to go to bed another night not knowing how he was doing.

The sound of the dime falling down the slot reminded her of a clock counting down to doomsday but she knew she had no choice.

"Hello?"

"Yeah, who's this?"

"I'm a friend of Nate. Is he there? I wanna speak with him."

"Hold on a second. Let me check. What did you say your name was?"

"My name *is* Gwen."

"Gwen, huh! Alright, let me check."

Gwen looked around the club and saw the group of women she was just speaking with, getting up to leave. She also noticed a young white woman with auburn hair come in and sit by herself at the bar. She seemed to be enjoying the band.

"Hello… yeah, he's here! Whaddya want with him?"

"I'm his girlfriend and I need to speak with him."

"Well, if you're his girlfriend, what's he doing here?"

"I don't know what he's doing there, but I need to speak with him."

"Listen, he ain't comin' home with you. You need to go on about your business, cause obviously he's not into you."

"Wait a minute! Who are you talking to like that?"

"I remember you now, Gwen. You're that short runt that used to hang around Jink! Well, he's here but he ain't going back to you. So, you can just forget it."

Before Gwen could respond, she heard the dial-tone.

She pondered for a second and realized it was useless calling back. She couldn't force him to do anything he didn't want to do.

She looked around over again at the empty booth, hoping the women would return but it was still empty. She pulled up a chair next to the young white woman at the bar.

They both smiled at each other. One of the guys from the band stopped the music and asked the crowd if anyone wanted to sing with the band. No one answered.

The band stopped playing, "No one!" Then the lead singer looked over at Gwen. "Hey, pretty lady… here's your chance to shine. I know a singer when I see one!"

The young woman next to Gwen said, "Are you a singer?"

"I hoped someday to be!"

"Well, give it a shot. You never know who's sitting in here?"

After some motioning by the band, Gwen got up and grabbed the mic. The band stopped the music and huddled for a few seconds. The guitarist shouted out a tune to Gwen.

"Yes! I know that one very well!"

On cue, the band ripped into an Isley Bros.' tune and for the next ninety-minutes, Gwen either fronted or sang co-lead for the band.

It was nearing the end of the night and the band gave Gwen a hug. One of the band members discreetly pushed some money in her hand before they started packing up.

"Will we see you again… Miss…"

"Gwen. Gwen Collins. Yes, I hope so. This was so much fun!"

"Okay, then Gwen Collins. We'll see you again… soon?"

Gwen nodded and walked back to the bar.

"You were great! By the way, my name is Vicky!"

"Vicky! Hi, again. Thank yo so much. I saw you dancing and everything. That really made me feel good. I know they're closing up soon but I gotta order something to go 'cause I'm starving."

Gwen unclenched the bills and opened her purse. As she counted all of her money, she knew she had to be modest in what she ordered. The money tonight would roughly extend her time about two more days.

"What's wrong, Gwen? Maybe, I can help?"

"You can't help me, but thanks anyways."

"How do you know I can't help?"

Gwen turned to face her. "I'm staying up the street at the the motel. I've been sick in bed for the past two days. Two days that I needed to be looking for a job and then I discovered my man ran off with some of my money to a junkie's house. That's not to mention that I have a child to support and Christmas is coming up and layaways and the rest of my expenses. So, I've got a lot to think about."

Vicky looked down to her feet, then looked up. "Hey, you wanna help me with a job tomorrow? It pays really, really well."

"Doing what?"

"Don't worry. It's really easy. I'll tell you tomorrow, if you're interested?"

"Okay, I'm intrigued. Where's it at?"

"I'll tell you all about it tomorrow. Let's meet here around noon? Is that good for you?"

"Twelve sounds fine."

"Okay, I'll see you then. And, I hope things work out between you and your boyfriend."

"Yeah," Gwen said softly. "Boyfriend."

31

She slumped into bed around 3:30 a.m. As she hit the pillow, she wondered how was she able to do this all the time when she was twenty. Those happy but crazy moments she spent with Jink morphed into the present with the spirit of Bosie looming over her mind.

Gwen laid in bed, staring at the ceiling. She hadn't looked at her watch but she guessed it to be around 9:30 a.m. She was still tired but happy. Remembering how the people were dancing and the applause she had received made her feel happy in a way that she hadn't felt in a long, long time.

"I have a long day ahead of me and my feet hurt," she thought. "What am I going to do about money? What kind of job does this girl do? I hope it's not selling drugs? What about Bosie? What about our plans?"

A knock at the door but before she could get up, the door opened. There stood Bosie.

The sight and smell of him flooded her senses.

"Stay right there! Don't come any closer," she cried.

"Why? I ain't good enough for you now? I messed up and now you want to disown me?"

"No, Bosie," holding her nose. "You stink! I can smell you from here. You're still wearing the same clothes you came here in and you're grimy."

"So what am I supposed to do? You got my clothes by you."

"Hey, go and take a bath. There's an extra toothbrush by the sink. I'll put some fresh clothes out for you, but we need to talk."

Bosie threw up his hands and walked down the hallway to the bathroom. True to her word, when he came out of the shower he found fresh, folded clothes on the toilet seat." Bosie walked back to the room wearing his favorite Lee jeans, blue Converse All-Stars, a V-neck undershirt. A short-sleeved shirt was draped over his right shoulder, while he dried his hair with a small towel with his left.

He looked down to see his suitcase and the tightly-knotted plastic bag containing his foul clothes.

"You wanna talk about it?"

"Yeah, I do," she said, as she took a sip of water and a couple of pills. "I trusted you. I believed in you. I believed in you enough to bring you down here. I loved you."

"So, you don't love me now? Well, that's okay. You ain't the first and you definitely ain't the last. I'm outta here!"

"Wait… aren't you gonna try to explain what happened?"

"Okay, since you so stuck on about knowing. Yeah, I was with her. I was going to pick up your medicine but I needed a drink. I remember seeing that bar and stopped in. That girl, Nancy, came by and one thing led to another and we did some Bam!"

Gwen was about to say something she knew she was going to regret but was interrupted when she heard him say, "Bam!" She smiled when she first heard the slang term as the street name for the drug, Preludin.

*** *** ***

Preludin," the brand name for the international drug called, Phenmetrazine, has been around since the early 1950's. It was created in Germany in 1952 and marketed throughout Europe starting in 1954.

Initially, an amphetamine used to treat obesity as an appetite suppressant, the drug was found to enhance the feelings of euphoria and heighten sexual arousal. During the 1970's, it was one of the top, underground drugs of choice.

It wasn't uncommon for street-workers to use and offer their customers *Bam* before the act went down.

*** *** ***

Bosie stared at Gwen for a moment. He knew without saying anything that it made no sense to feed her any lies, yet he was frustrated there was no way he could save face.

"I'm outta here. You can keep dreaming but I know what life's really about and it aint what you've been thinkin'"

Gwen held back, knowing if she let off all of his dirty business would be heard by anybody walking by the building.

"Don't let the door hit ya', where the Good Lord split ya."

*** *** ***

It was Gwen's turn to sit in the tub. She cupped her hands full of water and brought them to her face. Each time, she'd pressed her hands against her face, all of the water seeped through her fingers.

"Why is this always happening to me? Why? I'm a good person. Why do people always like to take advantage of me?" The same questions repeated themselves over and over in her mind.

Soon, she discovered the water was cold and she hadn't soaped herself. "Oh, my god, what time is it!" Ten minutes later, she was in her room getting dressed to meet Vicky at Spiro's. The thought of hanging out with a new friend and making some money provided her with a bit of an emotional upliftment.

Gwen walked into Spiro's, out of the breath. It was 12:05, but she wanted to take that extra few minutes to make sure that she didn't forget anything she thought she might need.

"Hey, Gwen!"

Gwen turned around and saw Vicky waving at her from the entrance.

"C'mon, I got the car running!"

Gwen was surprised to see Vicky in a mid-sized sedan: a faded, sky blue Chevy Chevelle. A pair of big, spongy dice hung from the rear-view mirror and several cassette tapes were scattered over the passenger seat.

"You can throw them on the floor if they're in your way. I didn't have time to clean. When I got home last night, I just fell out on the bed. What time did you get in?"

"Almost 3:30! I still couldn't believe how much fun I had. Did you have fun?"

"Gwen, girl, you were great! Who needs Diana Ross when we have you?"

Gwen was about to tell her about how she used to send cassette tapes to Ross and others in the industry and never got a response, but she decided in the last second to let the question die.

"By the way, where are we going? What am I gonna do and how much money are we getting? If you don't mind my asking?"

Vicky chuckled, fixing the driver's side outsider mirror.

"We're gonna see a friend."

"A friend! A friend or… a boyfriend," Gwen interjected.

"I don't know the difference." She looked at Gwen. "To be totally honest, he's a friend. And, we do *friendly* things."

"Friendly… things?"

"He and I have an understanding and that understanding doesn't have to be explained. He'll call and ask me what am I doing. I'll tell him if I'm busy or if I have time to talk. But because my parents' phone is not the best, I agreed that we'd talk in person at his house."

"Oh," Gwen said. "So, how does this involve me? Or, am I supposed to just watch the both of you…"

"No, not at all. I need you to carry a few things for me from his house to the car. That's it! Just a couple of bags and we'll be on our way"

"Carrying a couple of bags from the house to the car? That doesn't sound like you need another person. Is there something you're not telling me?"

"Gwen, it's alright! I'll tell you what. If you're not happy with what I pay you, you don't ever have to work with me again."

Gwen shook her extended hand.

*** *** ***

It wasn't ten minutes later that the Chevelle parked in front of a quaint two-story house. Nothing out of the ordinary: a large tree out front, a row of unkempt shrubs to the side of the house.

As the women got out of the car, Vicky turned to Gwen, "Hmmm, you might not want to lock it. It'll be easier if the door was unlocked. Oh, and another thing, just follow my lead. We won't be here very long, maybe just an hour."

Gwen shrugged her shoulders and walked behind Vicky.

Vicky walked up to the door and knocked twice in quick succession. The drape on the other side of the door moved over very slightly. The door opened very slowly.

In front of the women, stood an older man maybe in his late 60's. He stared at Gwen for a second but before he was able to speak, Vicky looked at him and then at Gwen. "This is my friend, Barbara. I'm giving her a ride back home. She cleans my parents' house. It'll be alright. She's won't say anything, she'll just sit down in the hallway while we talk."

His demeanor slowly changed. He looked to Vicky and said, "Well, if you say so, Karen. I trust you." He stepped to the side and fully opened the door for them to enter.

He was still wearing an old, dingy pajama bottom and a hole-ridden undershirt. The foyer was musty, like the smell of decades old newspapers and yellowing peppermint candies.

"Barbara," he said. "You can have a seat right over here. Pardon the mess, I just wasn't expecting extra company."

Gwen hesitated for a second until she realized that he was talking with her. "Thank you, sir!"

He walked into the room and Vicky started right after him.

"Give me a second, Mister Jim," She turned to Gwen in a louder than normal volume for such a close proximity. "Now, Barbara, I'm gonna help Mister Jim with his crossword puzzles and straighten out his closet. I won't be long, perhaps you can read a book if you get bored."

Gwen looked at her baffled.

Vicky moved closer and whispered in Gwen's ear. "Okay, you'll need to move fast and you cannot make any noise whatsoever."

"I'm not moving from here," Gwen said.

"No, you are! In about ten minutes. You're gonna go to that door and go to the basement. Over on the shelf by the window is an old box. Move that box and you'll see a large duffle bag. Take that bag and put it in the backseat of the car. Make sure you put everything back exactly where you found it. I should be done with him in fifteen minutes. You got it?"

"Yeah… I guess."

A few minutes passed and Gwen heard the expected grumblings inside the bedroom. She slowly got up and went through the secret door to the basement.

As far as the eye could see, the darkly lit room was cluttered with books, papers and boxes. Old paintings with inch-high dust adorned all four walls. The images, mostly faded with time, seemed to be direct relations with Mister Jim. She looked around frantically for the big box and the bag underneath but the jitters had her second-guessing her purpose. She took a deep breath and closed her eyes. She slowly opened them and saw the box and the bag.

She was tempted to look inside first, but wondered if she were caught with the opened box, could it spell time in Pence again.

She carefully crept up the stairs and as she was about to reach the top step, she noticed another bag, off in the corner. She felt the pull to see what was in that bag.

She got to the car and threw the bag in the backseat. When she got back in the foyer, she leaned into the bedroom door and it sounded like Vicky was finishing up. She knew it was now or never. She threw caution to the wind and raced downstairs.

This bag was noticeably heavier and bulkier than she reasoned. She heard the sound of metal rubbing against metal. Whatever was in there, she had to find out. Besides that, as she carefully picked up the bag, she realized that she was never coming back. So in the end, it wouldn't matter.

Vicky exited the room first just as Gwen returned from her second trip to the car.

"Barbara, are you ready to go?"

"Yes, Miss… Miss…"

"Karen! My name is Karen. Don't you know who you work for," Vicky said with a smirk.

"Well, Karen," the voice behind her called, "when do you think you'll be stopping back to play crosswords again?"

"Soon, Mister Jim. Well, we'll see you later."

"Nice to meet you, Barbara. You're welcomed to come back anytime."

Gwen waved at him and briskly walked to the car.

"I think I need a sedative for my nerves after all of this."

"You'll be fine," Vicky said as she sped through the side streets back to downtown Charleston.

*** *** ***

The women made it back to Gwen's motel and were lucky enough to find a parking space right in front of the door. Gwen carried the lighter bag and Vicky struggled with the last bag.

After they entered the building and were walking up the stairs to her room, Gwen turned to Vicky.

"What's this all about? You took me to that old man's place just to rip him off? What's so important about these bags?"

Vicky dropped her bag on the floor and took off her shoes and climbed on top of the bed. She crossed her legs and unzipped *Gwen's bag* and turned the bag upside down as the contents came tumbling out of the top.

To her surprise, Gwen saw stacks and stacks of fifty and twenty dollar bills. There was no denomination smaller than a ten.

"Oh, my god! Oh, my god! He's gonna kill us. Vicky, we can't keep this. He's gonna come looking for us."

Vicky said nothing but continued to separate the bills into two identical groups and had them in order of their amount size. Two rows of the exact same amount. She licked her fingers while counting and distributing the money until she came to the last bills.

"What's in the other bag, Gwen" Vicky said without looking up.

Gwen had completely forgotten about the heavy bag next to her feet. She muscled it up to an area of the bed that was untouched by Vicky. She unzipped the bag, turned it over and poured out its contents.

There was no money. There was nothing that carried money. There was nothing as green as money. The only thing in front of Gwen were guns. Guns, rifles and ammo. Some vintage firearms and some contemporary.

"You can have them," Vicky said glancing up. "I hate guns."

"How did you know he had all this money?"

"I don't go over there because I like to play crossword puzzles. It's a business transaction 101. He offers me money for my services. Now, sometimes, but not all the time, me might be in his so-called office downstairs working on his memoirs before we go upstairs to his bed.

"So, to directly answer your question. One time we had finished early and he asked me if I wanted to see some cool stuff that he had been collecting for decades. I said yes and while I was there, I found the bag with a stack of money. He was either talking to me with his back turned or he went to the bathroom and left me downstairs."

Vicky looked up at Gwen as she took one row of bills and put it in her bag. "Okay, the deal is 50-50! This line over here is for you. I hope you can take care of your needs without worrying so much."

Gwen was mesmerized.

Vicky smiled, "Ten thousand dollars for an hour's work. Not even the president makes that!"

Gwen could not sleep that night. Tossing and turning, getting up every couple of hours to check on the bags that had the money and the guns: it was all too much to take in for such a short period of time. It was only her last round, around 4:30 a.m., that she finally felt drowsy enough to sleep uninterrupted. At 10 a.m. sharp, she was wide awake.

She awoke with a mixture of fear and excitement. The exact same feeling she had when she did a shot of speedball. She replayed the moment Vicky gave her the go-ahead. It felt like she was watching a scene in an action flick except she was starring in it. And, why did Vicky think she looked like a *"Barbara?"* She cupped a handful of water in her hands and rinsed the toothpaste from her mouth.

She hid the money bag underneath the bed and grabbed the bag with the guns. If anyone would know what to do with them it would be her new friends from the band.

Stepping away from the motel, she put on some dark shades and looked around twice despite the last thing Vicky told her before she left. If you've been robbed of that much, would you go looking for it?

The band was playing at The Gentlemen's Club and were happy to see her again. They took a fifteen-minute break between sets to see what Gwen had brought them.

"Don't ask any questions," Gwen said to the guitarist. "It's a gift. My ex-boyfriend left it and and he's not coming back. I don't want it so you can have it."

"Are you sure he won't come back for this? People don't usually leave something like this."

"I'm sure. Besides, he took all of my money and left me stranded. You can take it and do whatever you want with it."

The guys looked at each other in confusion. "Alright, we'll take it. Can't promise that we can get anything for them but thanks."

"No, I don't want any money. You can keep them or you can pawn them. I just don't want them. I don't like guns."

Gwen left the podium and walked to an empty table to pick up a menu. She looked at her watch: it was almost 1 p.m. and she hadn't eaten anything all morning.

"Can I sit with you," a voice behind her said.

Gwen turned around and saw a familiar face. She knew her from somewhere but couldn't place it or her name.

"Gwen, don't you recognize me? It's me Mary Beth?"

"Mary Beth, oh my god! It's so good to see you. How long has it been?"

"Girl, I don't know. Ten years? What do you think?"

"That sounds about right. What are you doing here?"

I was driving by when I saw someone who looks like you wearing some dark shades and struggling to carry a bag. I wanted to give you a ride but them you disappeared. Well, how've you been doing?"

Gwen shook her head. "You don't wanna know. We don't have the time or the enough tissue paper to talk about it. Tell you what, why don't you pick out something on the menu and let have lunch. It's on me. I got paid yesterday."

"How about this," Mary Beth said as she adjusted her shoulder strap, "order three of what you're ordering and we'll take it with us. I want you to see my home."

"But, three?"

"Yeah! I've got a surprise. There's someone there you haven't seen in a long time."

*** *** ***

Despite what Gwen said about not having the time to reminisce, on the way to Mary Beth's house, she started talking about her history after she was arrested for probation violation.

Gasp's and stunned silence moments were frequent responses from Mary Beth. Occasionally, Gwen had to answer the questions, "How did you get through that?" "What happened after that?" "No, that couldn't have happened!" She realized then, it was easier to talk about those moments in the present than when it was actually going on.

They pulled up to the house. It was a beautiful house with a nice manicured lawn, peach colored exterior with white trim around the windows and door and a dark brown trim that accented the outline of the house. Inside pictures of Mary Beth's parents decorated the walls and the foyer leading to the living room. Just above the mantle, a picture of Mary Beth's father receiving his doctoral degree in veterinarian science.

A recliner in the other end of the room slowly turned in the direction of Mary Beth and Gwen: There sat Phyllis.

The women ate lunch, while laughing and crying about old times and old boyfriends. Gwen was also impressed to learn that Phyllis' uncle became a city councilman.

After the reminiscing had died down, Phyllis clapped her hands, "Hey, you wanna get high like old times?"

"Yeah," Mary Beth said.

They both looked at Gwen.

"I'm in. You don't have to ask me twice!"

Gwen listened to the exchange between the women, each stating that they didn't have enough money to make the trip to Ripley. It was during that conversation that Gwen remembered when she used to run the streets with Phyllis and how Phyllis was untrustworthy. She wouldn't show up when she said she would, if at all. She wouldn't come clean with the amount of money she made from a john.

It was all coming back to her.

"Gwen… Gwen," Mary Beth called.

"Oh, yes. My mind was elsewhere. What's up?"

"We were just thinking. I know you just bought us lunch but do you have any extra money we could borrow? Sometimes we go to Ripley to this Rite-Aid. We got a pharmacist who always fills our prescriptions but we need some money to actually pay for the pills. So, do you have it?"

Now, why would they make a big deal about getting high when they don't have any money? That doesn't make any sense. How much money do they think I got? "How much do y'all need? I'll see what I have left."

Phyllis came toward her. "Gwen, we just need a small investment. She's got these blank prescription forms from her father's office. I'll fill them out. Normally, we'd order a lot so we can sell the majority, make a profit and we'll keep the rest for us."

"Oh, so that's how you do it." Gwen looked in her purse, then realized she had a lot less than she thought. She was about to tell them but she saw the sparkle of her engagement ring from Bosie next to her keys. "I only have a couple of dollars on me but I can pawn my engagement ring and give you the money?"

Mary Beth and Phyllis looked at each other.

"Yeah!" And, "I suppose so," was said simultaneously.

"Okay, give me the ring, I'll go pawn it and come back."

"Oh, no! I need to go with you because I don't know if I'll see you two again. I want that ring. So, we can do this but we'll all go to Ripley. On the way, we'll find a pawn shop. We'll get the pills, you do your selling thing and you pay me back the money so I can get my ring. Deal?"

Mary Beth and Phyllis shrugged their shoulders.

*** *** ***

Mary Beth called her cousin to pick them up. She thought about the distance and the gas needed. It would also give the women time to strategize.

They pulled up to the Rite-Aid. Phyllis pulled the latch to the door next to her. "I'll be back in a few minutes. I promise I'll bring you back your change, Gwen."

A few minutes later, Phyllis came out of the drug store and got in the car and handed Gwen the change. "Look, Gwen, it's very simple. The guy we work with is on duty tonight. Just hand him the paper and if he asks you if you know who Dr. Chadwick is, tell him, Yes, he takes good care of my pets. That's it! Don't get into no long conversation. Get the pills and get out."

Gwen walked briskly to the entrance, feeling once again, the urgency of time and precision. She returned just a few short minutes later with a package in her hand.

Mary Beth went in next. Neither of the women said anything to each other or to Mary Beth's cousin.

Five minutes passed.

Ten minutes passed.

Then, a half-hour.

Gwen was about to comment when a police car drove into the parking lot and pulled up to the front door.

"We gotta go," Phyllis said to the driver.

"We can't go! What about Mary Beth," Gwen said.

"We gotta go. Let's go… DRIVE!" "NO! Don't go! We can't leave her!"

Phyllis turned to Gwen, "WE CAN'T BE HERE!" Then she turned to the driver, "LET'S GO!"

"NO! What about her? We can't go!"

Phyllis, again, turned to Gwen, "What's wrong with you? Are you crazy? What are you thinking? You wanna go inside and do what?"

"I don't know. I'll say something. We just can't leave her by herself!"

"She's caught! What don't you understand? We're about to get caught, too! YOU WANNA GO BACK TO JAIL?"

Gwen didn't respond but looked through her window to the entrance door of RiteAid.

"SIR, I AIN'T GONNA TELL YOU AGAIN, LET'S GET THE HELL OUTTA HERE. NOW!"

The car drove off and went a few blocks when they pulled into a gas station to fill up. There was a Long John's Silver restaurant a few feet away. They thought it might be a good idea to stop into

Long John's for a couple of hours before returning to Charleston.

Gwen went to the bathroom at the side of the gas station first. She needed to clear her head and come up with a strategy to clear Mary Beth, if she had been arrested but she knew Phyllis was right: She'd be headed right back to jail if she was connected.

She cracked open the door. She held her breath and looked through the slat hoping the coast was clear. She carefully opened it a bit wider. Again, waiting a moment to listen for some kind of activity.

When she was convinced she was safe, she walked out and walked to the parking area where the car was parked. The car was there. The doors were closed and the windows were down, but the driver and Phyllis was nowhere to be found. *They must be at Long John's,* she thought. She turned around and walked in the direction of the seafood restaurant when she heard the sound of a car driving slowly behind her.

She heard the engine but paid it no attention. *They could drive around me,* she thought.

All of a sudden, two high beams and flashing red and white lights came on behind her. It was so bright that Gwen could clearly see what was in front of her for an entire city block.

"GWEN COLLINS?"

She stopped and turned around.

"GWEN. GWEN COLLINS. WE KNOW IT'S YOU. STOP WHERE YOU ARE!"

"What do you want from me?"

Again, the blaring voice coming from the car's bullhorn said, "STAND RIGHT WHERE YOU ARE! WE WANT TO HAVE A WORD WITH YOU!"

Gwen covered her eyes, "What do you want with me? How do you know my name? I didn't do nothing!"

Two officers came out of the car with thick barrel flashlights. "Gwen Collins."

"Yes?"

"Where you just in the Rite-Aid a few blocks from here?"

As she was about to deny it, she saw Mary Beth and Phyllis in the backseat, "Yes, I was. I stopped in to get some aspirin for my headache."

"Anything else you went in for?"

"No."

"Well, unfortunately, we have you on the store's surveillance system. You were getting a prescription for a controlled substance."

"Oh, really! That wasn't me. I don't do drugs. I don't know anything about drugs! No, no. You've got the wrong person!"

"Be that as it may, you need to come down to the station with us. Spread your feet and place your hands behind your back."

None of the women said anything in the car on the way to the station. As they were escorted out of the car, one officer escorted Phyllis and Mary Beth and the other escorted Gwen.

They walked through a lobby where the first officer opened a door and led Phyllis and Mary Beth in. The second officer led Gwen to an open area with a lot of empty seats facing the Captain's podium.

"Miss Collins, we'll be with you in a few minutes. We don't have any available conference rooms ready yet."

Several minutes passed, when a police sergeant came in and grabbed a stack of papers behind the podium. He was about to leave when he noticed Gwen sitting by herself.

"My, my! What have we got here? What are you in for?"

She looked at him but said nothing.

"Oh, I see. Let me tell you one thing, Miss. We only ever had one niggra who lived in this here town and his name was Niggra Jim. And, we lynched him!" He walked off with a smirk.

Gwen suppressed the urge to call him a few colorful words, electing only to give him the middle finger as he turned the corner.

A moment later, two police officers came around the corner and stood in front of Gwen.

"Gwen Collins?"

"Yes."

"Please stand up."

"Are we going to one of the conference rooms?"

"Not quite, yet. We're here to tell you that you're under-arrest."

"UNDER ARREST! FOR WHAT? I DIDN'T DO ANYTHING!"

"You're under arrest for forgery and for being in possession of an illegal, controlled substance."

Praises For Gwen Womack

RanRan
5.0 out of 5 stars Very good reading about how one life was impacted in a small town
Reviewed in the United States on April 12, 2017
Verified Purchase
Being from the area MS. Collins was.born, I enjoyed her book immensely as I knew some of the people mentioned. Could not put this book and Second book down until finished. It ended to soon in her life. I do hope she continues her books and shows how her life continued and if she ever got her life back on track.

Trina R.
5.0 out of 5 stars WOW
Reviewed in the United States on May 3, 2016
Ok I expecting this book to be great, but it's exceptional!!!! I feel like I have a personal relationship with all the characters now. Great writing. It's get you to thinking about the life you had and have and it shows that no matter what you have been through you can achieve greatness when its your time. Waiting on book two!
Trina R.

Carlisha McKissic-Roberts
5.0 out of 5 stars The book you can't put down
Reviewed in the United States on November 4, 2016
I purchased this book as a gift for my mother. After she read the book she expressed how good it was. I had to know what was intriguing about this book. I also had to know about Gwen's life. This is a cousin I had known about, but never knew personally. I saw this as my way of knowing about the mystery behind this cousin of mine. She was the only one out of all of her siblings that I had never met. I opened the book and I couldn't put it down. I laughed, cried and worried my mom crazy asking about this person and that person in the book.

Family ties aside, this book is a MUST read! It takes you on an adventure and is depicted in a way that draws you into character. You not only take on Gwen's character, you take on Lila's, Cecil's, Michael's and numerous others. I look forward to reading book two and hope there are more. This would make an excellent Lifetime movie. Enjoy!

To Gwen: I simply want to say "thank you" for introducing yourself to me after 39 years of me being alive. I love you and love your spirit!

Mikki
5.0 out of 5 stars What an amazing, courageous walk through Gwen's life
Reviewed in the United States on December 9, 2015
What an amazing, courageous walk through Gwen's life... if you are looking for a book to ready and have a few hours? This a book that keep you turning pages waiting to find out what will happen to Gwen next.... Can't wait for the second book!

Amazon Customer
5.0 out of 5 stars AWESOME...LOVE LOVE LOVE!!!
Reviewed in the United States on December 12, 2015
What a great read?!!! This book captivated my attention from beginning to end, which is always a plus in my book! After I finished this book, I cried like a baby and I can't wait until the next one! Keep them coming!!!

DANA M.
5.0 out of 5 stars The heartfelt recollections of a young woman who loses innocence ...
Reviewed in the United States on February 3, 2016
The heartfelt recollections of a young woman who loses innocence, trust, and her way. Equal parts suspenseful and heart wrenching. Hard to put down!

Amazon Customer
5.0 out of 5 stars chapter 6 was enlightening
Reviewed in the United States on January 10, 2016
Chapter 6 was very emotional for me. I was saddened to learn that a person in the neighborhood that everyone knew and trusted was molesting the children.

Stephanie Hearne
5.0 out of 5 stars This book gives you a glimpse into an amazing persons life and its inspiring and it'll leave you ...
Reviewed in the United States on April 18, 2016
This book gives you a glimpse into an amazing persons life and its inspiring and it'll leave you wanting to know more.
-Stephanie H

Also by Gwen Collins Womack

ONE: A Journey Begins

TWO: Pain And Peril

THREE: Trapped Between Two Mountains

FOUR: Entrance To Exit [March, 2022]

FIVE: In The Free World Doing Time [July, 2022]

www.ingramcontent.com/pod-product-compliance
Lightning Source LLC
Chambersburg PA
CBHW031252290426
44109CB00012B/551